D0881121

LOGIC for
Undergraduates

LOGIC for Undergraduates

Robert J. Kreyche
University of Arizona

THIRD EDITION

HOLT, RINEHART AND WINSTON, INC.
New York   Chicago   San Francisco   Atlanta
Dallas   Montreal   Toronto   London   Sydney

LIBRARY
EMMANUEL SCHOOL OF RELIGION
ONE WALKER DRIVE
JOHNSON CITY, TN 37601

BC
108
.K7
1970

Copyright 1954, © 1961 and 1970 by Holt, Rinehart and
Winston, Inc.

All rights reserved
Library of Congress Catalog Card Number: 70-97844
SBN: 03-078095-0

Printed in the United States of America
9 8 7 6 5 4 3 2 1

To The Memory Of My Beloved Wife, Julie

Gift: Appalachian State Univ. Library

7-21-88

70958

Preface

Thanks to a wide range of students and instructors who have chosen to use this text, *Logic for Undergraduates* has enjoyed a long, steady period of growth since it was first published in 1954. When I first taught at Loyola University in Chicago, I conducted a variety of experiments in presenting logic to students, and from those experiments came the first edition of this work. Favorable response to the first edition encouraged me to enlarge and revise the text in 1960—at which time new sections were developed, such as those dealing with the logic of syllogistic construction and the techniques of induction. The use of the second edition was greatly facilitated by the publication of a workbook companion. However, by 1966 I felt the need for a total revision of both the text and workbook. Accordingly, from 1966 to 1969 I prepared a further enlargement of the scope of the book to make it more practical and appealing and to bridge the gap between traditional and modern logic. This volume, together with an entirely new workbook, is the result of that endeavor.

Chapter 1, a brief outline of the different uses of language, serves as a preparation for the remainder of the text even as logic itself is often regarded as a preparation for philosophy. Chapters 2 and 3 ("Sources of Deceit") offer an extensive presentation of fallacies. These chapters not only define the traditional lists of fallacies together with up-to-date examples, but provide a contemporary treatment of such new topics (new for most logic texts) as the "psychology of big names" and the use of slogans. The reader should note that the section on fallacies is near the beginning of the book rather than at the end—lest it be slighted, let us say, in the very last week or two of the course.

Chapter 4 seeks to integrate the study of judgment with critical thinking and the logic of making decisions. In any event, this chapter contains a variety of helpful reminders (see pp. 52–53) relative to the "art of making decisions." The chapters that immediately follow (5–7) stress, as did previous editions, the practical importance of handling categorical statements together with their various implications, such as obversion, conversion, and contraposition.

A major section of the remaining part of the book (chapters 8–11) deals with the logic of the categorical syllogism and practical argumentation. Throughout these sections emphasis is placed on judging the difference between authentic and pseudo-reasoning, identification of fallacies (see the new "box method," pp. 106–108), and the construction of logical arguments. A basic course in logic should not overlook the central importance of syllogistic reasoning (in relation to everyday discourse) as a method for making logic both relevant and humane.

Chapter 12 is a re-presentation of the logic of hypothetical inference with a particular emphasis on the use of modern symbolism. Throughout this chapter, examples have been chosen to enable the student to see the connection between the use of logical forms and their non-logical expressions in everyday use. Chapter 13 has been considerably expanded to include a more thorough study of the fallacies of induction together with Mill's basic canons. The final chapter, which is a new feature of this volume, provides a more technical introduction to symbolic logic, which may or may not be taken, depending on the needs of the course.

The reader will note that I have taken the bold step of developing the subject matter from within a philosophical tradition, namely that of a moderate realism, whch stresses the real basis in fact for all of our mental operations. This position (as opposed, let us say, to scepticism or nominalism) governs the entire movement of the text in its attempt to interrelate the study of logic as a discipline of the mind to the exigencies of the real world. Too, I have sought to establish the interrelationship between language and thought, and, more generally, between logic and life. The modern student must be able to cope with an incredible variety of dicta and slogans that are flung at him from all fields, and it is here that discrimination and sound judgment of the sort this volume highlights come into play. If logic is presented as just another discipline to be studied, just another requirement for a degree, then somewhere along the line, both teacher and writer have failed. It is the possibility of such a failure that I have tried to forestall in the writing of this text. I would like to recommend to any prospective user of this text the collateral use of the workbook companion. The workbook, both in its supplementary explanations and in the abundance of new examples it provides, has been specifically designed for use in conjunction with the text.

I have dedicated this book to my wife, who is recently deceased. Were she alive, she would be the first to whom thanks are due for her help and encouragement. Yet I wish to extend thanks as well to the members of the editorial staff of Holt, Rinehart and Winston, Jane Mayo and Elise Phillips. A special word of gratitude is extended for the unwavering help of my graduate assistant, George Godas, who is personally responsible for Chapter 14, and to Patricia Broome for her patience in typing the manuscript. Finally, a note of thanks is due to John Hof for the preparation of the index.

January 1970   *Robert J. Kreyche*

Contents

LOGIC for
Undergraduates

To the Student

What Logic Is Not
Logic as Science
Logic as an Art
What Logic Is

Few persons care to study logic, because everybody conceives himself to be proficient enough in the art of reasoning already. But I observe that this satisfaction is limited to one's own ratiocination, and does not extend to that of other men.[1]

Logic is a discipline intended both for the development of the understanding and for practical use. Logic is of use in everyday thinking, in study, in writing, in conversation, in speech, and in debate. But more will be said of this later; we must first inquire into the nature of the subject itself.

WHAT LOGIC IS NOT

Logic is not, as some people naïvely suppose, a panacea for intellectual deficiencies. Put to proper use, it is, of course, an instrument or a means for sound thinking. As such, logic puts order in one's thinking, but it does not on that account relieve one of the task of patient inquiry and research. The knowledge of logic is not, in other words, a substitute for *thinking through* a problem on its own merits—a streamlined method of "getting by with the least for the most."

A student once expressed regret that "logic does not solve *all* the problems of life"; he was puzzled to hear from his instructor that it does not

---

[1] Charles Sanders Peirce, "The Fixation of Belief," in Max Fisch, ed., *Classical American Philosophers,* New York: Appleton-Century-Crofts, 1951, p. 54.

solve *any* of them. This remark was intended, of course, to emphasize the fact that every problem must be met, with or without logic, on its own ground. While a knowledge of logic helps one to face a problem in a more orderly, systematic fashion and in many cases makes the solution less difficult and more certain, logic *of and by itself* does not solve problems, nor is it intended to do so.

No blueprint can take the place of a hammer or a saw, far less of a builder. But just as someone building a house should not work without a plan, the same holds true for the use of reasoning powers. If reasoning is merely casual or haphazard, it is apt to be erroneous. Logic seeks to prevent this type of thinking. In one respect its purpose is to see that human thinking, whatever the problem at hand, is not left to chance. In a more positive light, reasoning should terminate in knowing—just as drafting a blueprint should lead to building a house.

LOGIC AS SCIENCE

All science is knowledge of some sort, knowledge that is based on understanding a few basic principles and techniques. In this sense logic too—although it does not involve the use of laboratory equipment, microscopes, and the like—is a science. The unity of logic as a science derives from its single concern with directing our thinking processes to the achievement of their proper end, which is ultimately knowledge of the truth. A digression on the nature of logic as a science would be needless, but it will be helpful to remember the following points.

1. All science is basically a habit of mind, developed by training, research, and practice. Moreover, scientific knowledge enables us to judge and interpret certain facts (such as the fact that lightning strikes) in the light of other knowledge (such as the facts that lightning is electricity and that electricity can burn), and the same holds true of logic. Through logic we can judge, for example, whether a given line of reasoning, such as we find in a newspaper editorial, is valid and self-consistent or even whether, in the light of its premises, it is true.

2. Like most other sciences, logic too is a coherently organized "body of knowledge." However, the source of its unity and coherence is its dominant perspective—which is that of judging whether our thinking processes are consistent with each other and with certain objective standards of human thought.

3. As a science, logic has both a theoretical and a practical value. It has a theoretical value inasmuch as it helps us to understand our

mental acts and the principles that govern their use. It is practical insofar as we can apply what we have learned to everyday reasoning and discourse.

LOGIC AS AN ART

All art has something to do with "making"—whether with the carpentering of a desk, the construction of an art work on canvas, or even the making of musical sounds. When we raise the question, therefore, whether logic is also an art, we must ask, "What is it that logic makes?" Certainly logic does not in any direct way make money, or fame, or beautiful works of art. No doubt the easiest and simplest reply is that logic produces a certain kind of order or consistency in our thinking processes. Thus, someone who knows logic and puts it to use "makes"—or formulates—good definitions, sound implications, and valid reasonings and syllogisms. It is not my intent, however, to convey the impression that the use of logic is mechanical —as though the whole of it could be programmed into a computer. What we are concerned with here and throughout the book is the qualitative dimension of logic as one of the *liberal* arts.

Depending on how we divide the notion of "art," we get different categories of arts. For example, some arts are of a purely useful nature, such as the "art" of driving a car. Others, the fine arts, have an aesthetic value in that their sole purpose is the production of something beautiful. Yet logic does not belong to either of these categories. To call logic a "liberal" art is not to exclude its usefulness in, let us say, conversation and debate, but rather to emphasize that logic affects a person's intelligence. In short, it teaches him how to think.

No doubt all normal individuals have a certain natural capacity for thinking, and there is such a thing as *natural* logic. But logic is not natural in the sense that proficiency in using it can be acquired without practice. To use sound logic takes years of practice, together with maturity of mind.

A purely useful art has no other value than its immediate practical intent. Learning how to drive a car or to manipulate a sailboat may increase enjoyment of life, but these skills do not of themselves develop intelligence, nor are they intended to. A person may have an unusual skill, such as agility in climbing a steeple, but still remain narrow and uneducated. By contrast, the whole idea of a liberal art is that it develops the intelligence in such a way that it affects the entire person.

One other point: learning logic is not simply a matter of technical skill, but also one of understanding. This matter needs to be stressed in view of the fact that many works on logic today emphasize only its symbolic aspects, as though nothing else mattered. There is a tendency to devaluate logic in its ordinary human use—in critical thinking, solving problems, and detecting fallacies. This lack of sensitivity to the meaning of logic as a distinctly human discipline has prejudiced many young minds against it. This text, therefore, tries to achieve a balance in the study of logic between the technical aspects of the subject and the relationship it bears to the problems of life.

WHAT LOGIC IS

No one—not Aristotle, Francis Bacon, or John Dewey—has ever given a perfect definition of logic; in any case, it is unwise to begin a course with a rigid definition and then try to make the subject fit it. It is better for the student to discover for himself what logic is all about and in the end formulate his own definition. The following comments, however, may be of some preliminary help toward understanding the subject.

Logic and Philosophy

Though some controversy exists, most philosophers are agreed that logic is not, properly speaking, a subdivision of philosophy. The best way of stating the relationship is to say that logic is a "propedeutic" to philosophy—that is, a preliminary study that helps to prepare the way. For students who are not interested in learning more about philosophy, however, it should be said that logic can be studied as a subject by itself. In other words, the value of logic as a separate discipline can be realized independently of the theoretical questions that lie at the heart of philosophy, such as those that pertain to the origin of human knowledge.

Logic and Psychology

Logic and psychology partly overlap in what they study, but each subject examines its material from a different perspective. Both logic and philosophy are concerned with understanding our thought processes. But an important difference is that the psychologist is not interested, as the logician is, in how we *should* think. The psychologist wants to know how we actually do think and why. Thus, the psychologist's concern is mainly factual, whereas the logician is mainly interested in the norms, standards, and criteria of correct thinking. As a case in point, many practicing psychologists want to know why their patients think as they do with reference, let us say, to early childhood experiences, in the hope of effecting a cure. By contrast, the "therapy" of logic is not to produce "normal" individuals in the psychological sense of the term, but to help persons who are presumably normal to improve their habits of thought.

"Correct" Thinking

Logical standards, the canons of logical thought—call them what you will—are not as arbitrary as many people seem to think. In fact, all logic is based on judgments that are valid under any condition.[2] In this sense it is mistaken to think that there is a "Western" or "Eastern" logic, a Russian, Chinese, or American logic, insofar as it is wrong (logically—not morally wrong) for a person to contradict himself. For example, if I ask you whether you went to the store this afternoon, you are equivocating if you answer, "Well, in a sense I did, and in another sense I did not." With reference to this particular event (assuming that we both agree to the meanings of "store," "afternoon," and so forth), either you did or you did not. To say anything other is to create the faulty impression that "correct" thinking is like "correct" table manners. The use of the term "correct" has in each case a different sort of foundation: "correct" table manners are based on arbitrary custom, law, habit, and so on; "correct" thinking is based on a systematic use of the intelligence to describe and discover relationships in the world in which we live.

Order and Consistency; Validity and Truth

Much thinking today is done on the basis of whim, impulse, and purely subjective impressions. The expression "scatterbrained" pretty much describes the kind of thinking that is the opposite of logical thinking. Logical thinking requires that we take thoughts in *order,* that we discipline ourselves in following a certain "line" or progression of thought so that one thing follows in sequence from something else in such a way that a valid conclusion follows from its premises.

Logic is also concerned with *consistency.* The person who says one thing one moment and another the next is obviously inconsistent, and this criterion applies as well to our reasoning. We are consistent—logical—if our conclusions follow from our premises, and not otherwise. One can, of course, be consistently illogical, but that is another problem.

Finally, one of the chief concerns of logic is with the *relationship be-*

---

[2] The principle of noncontradiction is an example of one such judgment. Contradictory predicates cannot be simultaneously ascribed to the same subject: I cannot logically say or think that something is both a horse and not a horse at the same time.

tween validity and truth. An argument is valid whenever the conclusion follows—according to certain norms and standards—from what is stated in the premises. But not every *valid* argument leads to a conclusion that is *true*. For a conclusion to be true of necessity, the premises of the argument must be both valid and true.

Both the instructor and the student will now understand why we shall try to keep a balance throughout this text between a formalized approach to our subject and one that emphasizes the application of logic to ordinary life. On the one hand, there is no substitute for learning logic as a serious intellectual discipline, and this means learning it with all the scientific rigor the subject commands. Yet too scientific and technical an approach to our subject can readily obscure its use as a human instrument—for critical thinking, problem solving, the avoidance of fallacies, and the like. It is the combined theoretical and practical approach to our subject that this text will stress throughout.

chapter 1

Logic and Language

The Functions of Language
Language and Abstraction
Words and Terms
Terms and Their Use
The Extension of Terms
Definition

The purpose of this chapter is to acquaint the reader with some of the preliminaries for the study of logic, such as the different functions of language, the meaning of abstraction, and the question of terms and their use. The concluding section deals briefly with definition and the rules that govern its use.

THE FUNCTIONS OF LANGUAGE

In recent years much attention has been given to the study of language in its relation to logic, and this is all to the good because of the intimate relationship between our habits of thinking and the methods whereby we express our thoughts. Neither language nor logic should be considered as a frozen mold totally isolated from the other, and for this reason we list some of the ways in which language may be used:

1. expressive
2. suggestive
3. explanatory
4. interrogative
5. descriptive

Expressive Language

The expressive use of language is best illustrated in poetry—whose chief intent or concern is not with scientific truth, but with richness and depth of feeling. The importance of knowing this function of language is to prevent us from dissecting, let us say, a poem, such as Eliot's *Waste Land,* from a purely logical point of view and in a manner that would be irrelevant to its intent.

Frequently, too, in ordinary life situations we utter such expressions as "What a glorious sunset!" Given the circumstances of utterances such as these, it is irrelevant, if not insolent, for someone to give us a lecture on the inaccuracy of our expression because the sun does not really set. Expressive language should be taken for what it is meant to convey—nothing more or less.

Suggestive Language

Most often language is used simply as an instrument, not to express truth or falsity, but to advise, exhort, threaten, prohibit, or command. The purpose of this use is in some way or other to move a person to act (or not to act) on what we say.

Explanatory Language

The explanatory function of language is to relieve one's curiosity, wonderment, or even fear. A child awakens in the middle of the night, frightened at the thought that something evil has entered the room. The mother turns on the light to reassure the child that his fear is unfounded and that he suffers only from a bad dream. In its explanatory function the use of language may range all the way from primitive myths to the most sophisticated types of scientific explanation. Although in certain contexts an explanation may be considered true or false, it is far better to consider it "incomplete," "inadequate," "comprehensive," "adequate," and so on.

Interrogative Language

One of the basic functions of language is to ask questions about what we do not know, and part of the business of logic is to train us to ask the right kind of questions. Among the pitfalls to be avoided are "context-free" questions. For example, it makes sense to ask the question "What time is it?" only in the context of a particular time zone and of a specific method for determining time. But to ask, "What time is it, in general?" is to pose a meaningless question.

Special attention should be drawn here to the fallacy of complex question, as embodied in this sentence: "How often do you rob the local banks?" Questions like this may make sense in a given context, but they make assumptions that most of their potential responders are hardly prepared to admit.

> *Note:* Frequently language is used in an interrogative form with the intent of making a statement. This device is commonly known as the *rhetorical question.*
>> *Example:* Can anyone doubt that I am the candidate best qualified to become mayor of this city?

Descriptive Language

When we describe a situation, we utilize statements that are fundamentally true or false, for the following reason: descriptive statements either conform or do not conform to a state of affairs that exists in the outside world. If they conform, they are true; otherwise they are false. Statements of this sort are of utmost concern to logic, and they will be fully explained in subsequent parts of the text.

EXERCISE 1.1

A. Examine each of the following:

1. A little girl asks her mother, "Who made me?" (Discuss more than one context in which the mother might answer this question.)
2. John tells Mary that he would walk to the end of the earth to prove that he loves her. Suppose that Mary asks him to start walking, in what way has she misunderstood the function of language, or has she understood correctly?
3. Where does your smile go when you stop smiling?
4. Is the new Mayor of Atlantis a soccer player?

B. Draw up a list of your own examples, indicating the different functions of language as outlined in the previous pages.

LANGUAGE AND ABSTRACTION

Fundamentally every language is: (1) a system of sensible signs (2) that is dependent for its meaning on abstraction (3) and is established by convention or use. In calling language a system of sensible signs, all we are saying is that in using a language you are using something you can hear or see, or, in the case of Braille, feel. But hearing, seeing, or feeling is not enough to understand what a language means; for this, you also need abstraction.

For the purposes of this text we may define abstraction as a process by which we develop a meaningful awareness of the objects of our experience. Applied to the concept of language, this means that through abstraction we get beyond words as words to an understanding of the meaning or meanings they are intended to convey. When, for example, we hear such words as "voice," "spacecraft," or "desert," we not only grasp these words with our senses, but we perceive what they mean through our intellectual power of abstraction.

As to the final point: the various words we use to express ourselves in language are not natural, like a hiccup or a cough, but the result of convention or usage. This is to say that social convention is the source of the meanings we attach to the words we use.

WORDS AND TERMS

As Gertude Stein might have said, "A word is a word is a word"; but since words by themselves are meaningless, the problem is to know the difference between a *word* and a *term*. Quite simply, a term is a word or a group of words that has meaning, such as "rabbit," "Pacific Ocean," and "breeze." By contrast, such words as "of," "the," and "and," are mere connectives, having no independent meaning. For purposes of logic our chief interest, then, is not in words as words but in words as terms.[1]

Terms normally signify an object of thought through abstraction; that is, they signify something through the thoughts and ideas that are in our mind—*they do not signify objects by themselves*. Terms are sensible, *conventional* signs, unlike concepts, which are *natural* signs of their objects and as such do not significantly vary from one society to the next. Whether we use the German word *"Buch"* or the English word "book" to signify an object, our *concept* is the same.

EXERCISE 1.2

A. Decide which of the following are just words and which are terms.

1. to
2. the fellow who cheated me out of last week's wages
3. chair

---

[1] Note that a term may be either simple or complex. A simple term consists of only one word, such as "elephant." A complex term consists of a variety of words, such as "the man who lives downstairs."

4. both-and
5. something red

B. Which do you think are *natural* and which *conventional* signs?

1. "70 degrees Fahrenheit" as indicating a certain temperature
2. a smile as a sign of pleasure
3. "hippopotamus" as a sign of a certain type of large animal
4. your idea of blue as signifying that kind of color
5. smoke as an ordinary sign of fire

TERMS AND THEIR USE

Having made the point that every term, as a term, has an object, we must now take up the study of the use of terms—the way they function either as the subject or the predicate of a proposition. Quite simply, the subject is what we are talking about, and the predicate is what we say about our subject. As for the different *senses* in which terms are used, we make a fundamental distinction between univocal, equivocal, and analogous uses.

Univocal Use

If a term is applied to two or more objects in the same basic sense, then the use of the term is *univocal*. The following are examples of the univocal use of terms: "automobile" applied to Ford, Chevrolet, Ferrari; "book" applied to an encyclopedia and a paperback; "ocean" applied to the Atlantic and the Pacific.

Note: Of particular importance to logic is the fact that all class names are univocally predicable [2] of the members which comprise their extension. Thus, the term "plant" as applied to different kinds of vegetation (tree, shrub, rose) is univocally predicable of these different kinds of vegetative life. Or again, applying the term "tree" to elm, oak, or maple is to apply it in an identical, univocal sense.

Equivocal Use

We use terms equivocally when we apply them to two or more un-related classes of objects without any likeness of meaning. The term "dolly" in one context might be taken as an affectionate name for a doll; in another, it might mean a vehicle for carrying heavy objects. Since there is no correla-

---

[2] "Predicable" in logic means "what may be said of."

tion of meaning in the two uses, the term is said to be used in an equivocal sense.

In general, the equivocal use of terms involves meanings that are both different and unrelated, and it is a mere accident of language that we use terms in such a way. Thus, it is merely by chance that the term "ruler" means a person who governs a country and, in an altogether different context, a measuring stick. Imagine, therefore, how absurd it would be to reason in some such fashion as this:

> Every *ruler* has authority.
> Some measuring sticks are *rulers*.
> Some measuring sticks have authority.

Such an example is based, as many puns are, on sheer equivocation.

Analogous Use

We use a term analogously when the meanings we employ are different though somehow related. This is to say that the analogous use of terms involves a partial, not a total, shift of meaning. In the sentences "Man is a technological animal" and "A man is ordinarily stronger than a woman," the term "man" is used analogously. In each sentence the term "man" is used in a different sense, yet this difference is not so radical as to result in a complete shift.

One of the most common instances of the analogous usage of terms is the metaphor. It is a curious fact, for instance, that men apply the names of many different animals—such as "fox," "beaver," "lion," "tiger," "shark"—to their fellowmen, in accordance with the characteristic they wish to stress. However, not every instance of the analogous use of a term is metaphorical. There are different kinds of analogy, of which the metaphor is the most obvious.

In testing for the sense in which a term is used we should first ask whether its meaning, when it is applied to different objects, is basically the same. If it is, then the term is used univocally. On the other hand, the equivocal use of terms involves a complete shift of concepts. Finally, the analogous use of terms involves concepts that are different but in some sense related. We may take this to mean that the analogous use of terms presupposes concepts which, though different, are in some way alike in their intention.

EXERCISE 1.3

Determine whether the following italicized terms are used univocally, equivocally, or analogously:

1. feeling *well;* a deep *well* of water
2. *cross,* referring to one's disposition; sign of the *cross*
3. *bunk,* referring to an army bed; *bunk* as a slang term for nonsense
4. this course is a *breeze;* the *breeze* from the ocean
5. price *ceiling; ceiling* of a room
6. *bank* of a river; downtown *bank*
7. *leap,* as a jump; *leap* year
8. *gas tank,* with reference to a car and a truck
9. Russell and Heidegger are *philosophers*
10. *fakir* and *faker*

THE EXTENSION OF TERMS

The extension of a term is the application of it in a given proposition to *all, some,* or *only one.*

Universal Terms

A *universal* or *distributed* term is one which, as used in a proposition, is applied (whether affirmatively or negatively) in its *complete* extension. It is *distributed* to all the members of a given class.

Examples:
All men seek happiness.
No plant is capable of speech.

The usual signs of universal extension are such words as the following:

all	whatever	no
each	whoever	none
every	any	no one
everyone	anyone	nobody
everything	anything	nothing

Particular Terms

A term has *particular* quantity or extension when it is applied to an indeterminate portion of a given class.

Examples:
Some countries are ruled by dictators.
Certain people do not exercise their right to vote.

If any one of the following or like signs of quantity is prefixed to a term, it should (for purposes of logical treatment) be regarded as particular:

a few	very many
almost all	most
many	practically all

Singular Terms

The extension of a term is *singular* if the term applies to only one specified object, whether that object be a person, place, thing, or event.

Examples:
Abraham Lincoln
Washington, D.C.
the largest telescope in the world
the discovery of America

Collective and Divisive Terms

Terms may also be used either *collectively or divisively*. A term is taken collectively when the predication made applies to the subject *considered as a group or a unit* and not to the individuals that come under its extension. Take the proposition

All the angles of a triangle are equivalent to two right angles.

Here the predication "equivalent to two right angles" is made in such a way as to apply to the subject taken only as a unit, and not to the three angles taken separately.

On the other hand, a term is used *divisively* when the predication made applies to each individual coming under the extension of the subject term.

Examples:
The girls in our family have blond hair.
The members of our team are six feet tall.

In these examples the predicate is applied to each of the members falling under the extension of the subject.

Occasionally it is difficult to decide whether the subject is to be taken in a collective or a divisive sense.

Example: The audience applauded vigorously.

In an example of this sort one should take the statement in its most obviously intended sense. Although it may possibly be true that each and every member of the audience applauded vigorously, it is also a fact that, even if one or two members refrained, the statement itself would remain true. The most obvious intended sense of this proposition is a collective one.

EXERCISE 1.4

A. Make your own list of the usual signs of universal and particular extension. Give examples of singular terms.

B. Tell whether the following italicized terms are to be taken collectively or divisively.

1. We're *all* "loaded down" with class work.
2. *Each of us* is required to study.
3. *Our team* won the top award for football.
4. *Spaghetti and meatballs* make a fine dinner.
5. *The potatoes in this barrel* weigh 200 pounds.

C. Make up some of your own examples.

DEFINITION

One of the functions of logic is to avoid confusion, and a highly useful device toward this end is definition. The purpose of definition in general is to mark off the subject-to-be-defined from all other subjects. In logic we refer to the subject-to-be-defined as the *definiendum* and to the definition itself as the *definiens*.

Of the various types of definition, note especially the *stipulative* or *nominal* definition, whose purpose is to define the meaning or use of a term as such. Very often, for purposes of a particular discussion or context, we find it necessary to indicate how we intend to use a certain term: "By 'political party' I mean any type of political organization that is officially represented on the ballot."

As for the method of defining, the best and most common one is that of *genus* and *difference*. By genus is meant some wider class to which the subject belongs.

> *Examples:*
> Plant: a kind of organism
> Telephone: a means of communication
> Garage: a type of structure

Our next step is to set forth that characteristic which most sharply distinguishes the *definiendum* from all other members of its genus.

> *Examples:*
> Man is a rational animal.
> An organism is a living thing.
> An ash tray is a container for holding such items as cigarettes and cigars or for dumping ashes.

The rules of definition may be stated quite simply as follows:

THE DEFINITION SHOULD BE COEXTENSIVE WITH THE DEFINIENDUM. This means that the definition should be neither too narrow ("Happiness is having a picnic") nor too broad ("Happiness is a state of mind").

THE DEFINITION SHOULD NOT BE CIRCULAR. Don't define an object in terms that fail to get beyond the language of the thing to be defined: "A professor is someone who professes something."

THE DEFINITION SHOULD BE EXPRESSED IN POSITIVE TERMS. One can discourse endlessly about what a thing is not; say what it is.

THE DEFINITION SHOULD BE SIMPLER THAN THE THING DEFINED. Avoid definitions that are more complicated than the *definiendum*.

EXERCISE 1.5

A. Look up five dictionary definitions and discuss the elements that go into their making. Try to identify any uniform patterns or techniques that are used.

B. Discuss the following definition:

> "Dialectic" is a convenient technical name for the kind of thinking which takes place when human beings enter into dispute, or when they carry on in reflection the polemical consideration of some theory or idea.[3]

C. Using the method of genus and difference, define the following:

1. banquet
2. submarine
3. helicopter
4. detective
5. sonnet

---

[3] Mortimer Adler, *Dialectic,* New York: Harcourt, Brace & World, 1927, p. 5.

chapter 2

Sources of Deceit I
Linguistic Fallacies

How to Approach This Study
The Definition of Fallacy
Fallacies of Language
The Psychology of Big Names
Slogans and Their Uses

HOW TO APPROACH THIS STUDY

Throughout this volume we shall try to develop a consciousness in the reader of the importance of critical thinking—the kind of thinking that involves a reflective awareness in evaluating the use of terms, propositions, and arguments. At the very outset of our study we shall put to use all the techniques of logic to make critical thinking a reality rather than a mere ineffectual wish. But before we proceed, a few words of caution are in order.

1. In your study of this and the following chapter, do not look for a complete and exhaustive list of the names of every type of fallacy. The conventional list of names is just that—a conventional list that allows for indefinite possibilities of expansion. We should not restrict ourselves only to that list; the business of sorting out bad methods of reasoning should allow us enough free play even to discover, if necessary, a few fallacies of our own, whether they have preferential names or not. Nor should one hesitate to assign new names where the old ones are inadequate.

2. Most teachers, students, and authors despair of finding some ideal list of fallacies that is foolproof from the standpoint of logical division. The cause of this failure lies in the inherent difficulty of the subject matter itself. As one author has remarked, the informal fallacies defy perfect classification

precisely because they are informal, and because some of them pertain as much to the area of psychology as to that of logic. This does not mean that no division can be made, but that all divisions of fallacies are imperfect. In practice, most informal fallacies tend to overlap. Accordingly, as you work out your examples of fallacies, be content to specify the one that pre-dominates—with the understanding that others may be present as well.

3. A third point of caution: Some persons tend by nature to be "witch hunters" in the sense that they are inordinately suspicious of the validity of *any* argument or point of debate. To forestall this unfortunate habit, one should avoid the temptation of crying "fallacy" at the slightest suspicion that something may be wrong with an argument. One should not be pre-disposed to "jump" on his adversary's argument with a set of fallacies, as though they were to be used as so many weapons in debate. It is one thing, after all, to be "critical" in a constructive sense and quite another to be so captious as never to concede a point in favor of the person with whom one chooses to disagree. Our study of fallacies, then, should not be infected with the frame of mind in which we pedantically display a minimal knowl-edge of logic to the total neglect of anything valid that another person has to say or offer. As much as anything else, the purpose of this chapter is to create an awareness of deficiencies in reasoning wherever they exist, whether in others—or, as the case may be, in ourselves.

THE DEFINITION OF FALLACY

One of the advantages of studying fallacies at this point is that it gives us a head start in the practical aspects of handling logical arguments prior to the technical study of the syllogism. If the student follows this pro-cedure, he will be able at the very beginning of his course in logic to identify by name some of the most common fallacies that arise in everyday discus-sion and argument. He will also have the advantage at the very outset of his course of spotting defective arguments in his everyday reading material, such as the newspapers and magazines.

Further, there is a special advantage in studying this chapter on lin-guistic fallacies as a direct sequel to the chapter on logic and language. We shall be able to put to immediate use some of the distinctions learned in the previous chapter concerning the use of terms, such as the distinction between their collective and divisive use.

Our preliminary study of fallacies will be limited to what are known as informal fallacies—those that can be learned prior to any technical study of the syllogism. At a later stage of the book we shall also study the formal fallacies of the syllogism and the fallacies of induction. Finally, in this and the following chapter we shall expand our approach to the subject of fallacies to include in some detail such practices as the use of slogans and the psychology of big names. All of these subjects—which receive insufficient attention in most logic texts—are an integral part of the logic of critical thinking.

The term "fallacy" as it appears in ordinary usage has a meaning so broad that it defies definition. What the "man in the street" understands by "fallacy" is any kind of error, prejudice, mistaken impression, or illusion. In its more restricted logical meaning a fallacy is generally taken to be an *argument which, although having some semblance of validity, is actually inconclusive.* Accordingly, a fallacy is not primarily a mistake in judgment, but a mistake in reasoning. It is a mistake in reasoning which most often leads to a false judgment.[1]

For purposes of our treatment of the subject we shall include under our general title "sources of deceit" both fallacies—as taken in the strictly logical sense (mistakes in reasoning)—as well as other sources of deceit that may not be reducible to a fallacy.

FALLACIES OF LANGUAGE

The mistakes that arise through the faulty or improper use of language are innumerable. The traditional list of such mistakes should be of considerable help to the reader, however. They are equivocation, amphiboly, composition, division, and accent.

Equivocation

The fallacy of equivocation is generally considered to be a mistake in reasoning that arises through the faulty use of a single term in an argument. Suppose, for example, you reason that because a lawyer is "questioning the facts," he is being unreasonable. The hidden premise of your argument is that anyone who questions facts is unreasonable. Reasonable as this view may sound, the question as to whether the argument is valid or not depends on the use of the phrase "questioning the facts." The source of deceit in this argument, therefore, lies in the term "questioning the facts." In one sense it could mean "questioning the facts that are established" (which *would* be unreasonable) or merely "questioning something that is *alleged*

---

[1] It is generally maintained that a *fallacy,* as opposed to a sophism, is an *unintentional mistake* in reasoning, while a *sophism* is a misreasoning *deliberately calculated* to deceive. Whatever the merits of this distinction from a psychological point of view, it is preferable from the standpoint of logic to include under the term "fallacy" any mistake—unintentional or deliberate—in reasoning.

to be a fact." The latter type of questioning is entirely reasonable, and the validity of the argument depends on how the term is used.[2]

Amphiboly

In contrast to equivocation, amphiboly is a type of mistake that can arise through a faulty grammatical construction. In other words, amphiboly is a case, not just of a faulty term in an argument, but of an entire sentence that is ambiguous as it stands. Suppose, for example, that you are driving along the highway and see this ad in front of a road side restaurant:

Nickie's

One of our hamburgers is all you can eat.

It might be far-fetched to consider this statement as a fallacy, but insofar as it could lead to faulty reasoning on your part, it might well be taken as a source of deceit. The statement as it stands could be taken to mean that one hamburger is so rich and satisfying that you would not want to eat another—even, let us say, if it were given to you free. On the other hand, the statement has enough latitude to allow for another interpretation far less favorable to the consumer—in which case a careful second reading might save you the discomfort of indigestion and a dollar that is poorly spent.

> *Example:* This flood is the worst disaster we have witnessed since I became governor of this state.

Unfavorably read, this statement as it stands could be taken to mean that the election of the governor was itself a tragedy that was second to none.

Composition

As a fallacy, composition means that (1) you make a statement of one or more parts or members of a class and (2) proceed to apply that statement to the class as a whole. A classical modern example of this fallacy is illustrated by the many types of appeal used to get people to buy on the

---

[2] A more extended analysis of the fallacy of equivocation will be taken up subsequently, in the theory of the syllogism, under the *fallacy of four terms,* which is most frequently exemplified in the *fallacy of the ambiguous middle.* It is sufficient for the reader at this point to show that terms often shift their meaning within the course of a single argument.

installment plan. The line of reasoning is that you can afford to pay twenty-five cents a day to buy a second television set, to take out a loan to travel now and pay later, to buy a new automobile, and so on. The fallacy in this line of appeal lies in the neglect on the part of the consumer to consider that, although his limited budget might sustain one or the other of these plans, it cannot sustain all of them for an indefinite period of time.[3]

> *Example:* You and I and all of our friends are rich, and we all belong to the local Rotary Club. So the local Rotary Club must be rich.

In this, as in all such examples, we should note that what is true of the parts as such need not be true of the whole.

Division

The reverse of composition is division—the fallacy of thinking that what is taken collectively in one premise may be applied divisively in the other so as to lead to a valid conclusion. Such a conclusion, however, is invalid as is evidenced in the following example:

> Because you belong to a fine family, you consider yourself as an individual to be a fine person.

Or on a more expanded basis:

> My family is one of high moral calibre.
> I am a member of that family.
> So I am a person of high moral calibre.

It may turn out that you are the black sheep.

This fallacy is the *reverse* of composition because it assumes that what is predicable of a given whole as such is also predicable of each of its parts. But is this really the case? Here we have to draw a careful distinction in our interpretation of the words "whole" and "parts." If the whole in question is, let us say, a genuine class or species (man), then it is perfectly legitimate, on the basis of some predication we make of the whole, to predicate the same thing of the parts. Thus

> All men are persons.
> John is man (has the nature or essence of "man").
> So John is a person.

---

[3] In view of the quick jump from the "some" to the "all," note the close similarity between this fallacy and the inductive fallacy of hasty generalization (Chapter 14).

As a matter of fact, the entire theory of the categorical syllogism depends on the value of moving from the predication of the whole to the predication of the parts which belong to that whole.[4]

The fallacy of division, then, lies *in supposing that every whole is a natural class or species*. Relative to one of the examples above, the term "family" signifies a whole that is made of physical, not of logical parts. Thus "mother," "father," "son," "daughter" are parts of the family, but not in the sense that I can predicate family of each or any of these parts as is the case, let us say, of organism, man, plant—applied to individual organisms, men, or plants. The difference here is that a logical whole (see Chapter 9), is an authentic universal that is abstracted from its parts and is predicable of them. Not so in the case of a physical whole: "family" is not abstracted from any individual member of the family *but is a concept that applies to all the members taken together*.

Examples:
1. Our public library is one of the finest in the country. This book is part of the library, so it is one of the finest in the country.
2. Our team performed gloriously today. Since I as a member of the team played right field, I too played a glorious game.

Accent

In its most restricted meaning, the fallacy of accent is one that gives rise to a difference of interpretation through misplaced emphasis upon a syllable, word, or phrase in a sentence. Anyone who is familiar with the various techniques of speech—inflection, pause, emphasis—is in a position to know how readily the meaning of a statement can be changed by the manner in which the sentence is uttered by the speaker. When a mistake in reasoning arises as a result of a change in meaning caused by such techniques, we have a fallacy of accent. If, for example, a woman buys a lottery ticket on the grounds that "one man will win" and later, having won the lottery, is disqualified on the grounds that one *man* would win, the fallacy in question would be one of accent—caused by a misplacement of emphasis.

The above example is somewhat trivial; it is of much greater importance for purposes of our study to know that the fallacy of accent may be applied, by extension, not merely to atomic words or phrases—taken, that is, out of context—but to entire sentences, paragraphs, and even speeches.

---

[4] A more expanded treatment of this point is taken up in the study of the categorical syllogism in Chapter 9.

In this more extended meaning of the fallacy we may well be justified in calling it by one or more names, such as the *fallacy of misplaced emphasis* or the *fallacy of distortion of meaning.* Yet by whichever name we call it, the fallacy consists either of "putting words into our opponent's mouth" or of using words that he actually uttered but according to a different meaning or context than that of their original intent.

Here the reader will recall the adage that the devil himself quotes scripture to his own advantage, as when one suggests, for example, that the expression "it is good for us to be here" applies to any and all situations— regardless of the circumstances to which they are meant to apply. Here the important consideration is that language is a living thing, a tool, an instrument for communication; under all circumstances its meaning must be established in relation to the context in which it is used. To fail to do so is to commit oneself to the fallacy of accent.

> *Example:* Two years ago Jeff said he wouldn't buy a new tractor because his old one was "good enough." Well, last month he changed his mind and bought a new one after all. How inconsistent can a farmer be?

EXERCISE 2.1

Determine as best you can the fallacy latent in each of the following:

> 1. This citrus farmer has one of the finest orange groves in the country. Therefore you can be sure that any bag of oranges you buy from him is of the highest quality to be had.
> 2. Most of the students I know who attend this university are wealthy. The university must therefore be wealthy.
> 3. All of the books in my library are well read. I too am well-read. Therefore there isn't much difference between me and my books.
> 4. Young people are inexperienced. Well, most old folks are young at heart. Therefore they too are inexperienced.
> 5. Presidential hopeful: "I do not choose at this time to run for the presidency." (Discuss ambiguities in this statement.)
> 6. It is hard for me to see how my neighbors and I can be blamed for discrimination when it comes to deciding who is to live in our neighborhood. We make discriminations all through life. If people are not allowed to discriminate, how can they make decisions in life between good and bad?

THE PSYCHOLOGY OF BIG NAMES

We have just seen a rough sketch of some of the traditional linguistic fallacies. We should hardly be doing justice to our topic, however, if we failed to consider what a profound impact names, images, and slogans—through the media of mass communication—exert on our lives. The various devices of the "communication industry" are the product of a vast industrial complex whose intent is to get the prospective consumer to respond positively to the desired product, whether that be a loan, a facial cosmetic, an electrically operated toothbrush, or the latest-model automobile.[5]

On what basis, then, do we make the decisions—economic decisions included—that significantly govern our response to the product we are persuaded to buy? No doubt the appeal of names has a measure of relevance but this relevance must be carefully weighed against the evidence at hand. As a case in point, one might normally assume that a distinguished cast of "big-name" actors is solid grounds for recommending a movie or play to the public. But is this necessarily the case? Frequently the worst movies are those that are glutted with talent—as a poor substitution, for instance, for a story with a good plot. In all such instances one might suspect a hidden use of the fallacy of composition as it was explained a few pages back: because a famous "name" leads the cast of this movie or play, the movie or play itself will be outstandingly good.

Nor must it be thought that the "logic" of "big names" is restricted to the entertainment industry alone. As most students know, a "big name" in the academic field is hardly the best recommendation for a teacher, and perhaps there should be a special name for the fallacy which assumes that a "big name" in research is the highest recommendation for the teaching "industry" as such. Equally, most often committees making lecture assignments are guided more by the thought of the "big name" than by the thought of the specific needs and intents of the local audience. A "big name" speaker may be too rich for a small audience or vice versa, in the sense that a small discriminating audience may be justifiably unimpressed by a big name that has nothing but popularity to commend it.

In the business world also "big names" ("personalities," "glamor attractions," and so on) may or may not be irrelevant. True, a well-established "brand name" is often as safe a guide as any other for determining

---

[5] Here reference should be made to the impact of nominalism within our society. By "nominalism" we mean the illogical tendency to accept slogans and names as arguments in themselves—in contrast to the practice of using one's rational and critical faculties as a means of making decisions. See also Chapter 4 on the logic of making decisions.

whether a product is of any value or not. But here, too, caution should be the order of the day. One reason is that we often pay a premium for a name that is sustained only by heavy advertising campaigns. Secondly, quite often the name stays the same, while changes in the product do not always effect improvements. Many a consumer of beer, for example, has discovered unhappily that what was once his favorite brand has become a watered-down version of the original, while the name has stayed the same.

Whether, then, in politics, entertainment, business, or any field you choose to select, you should guard against the tendency to accept "big names" or "brand names" for their surface value. Even more, you should guard against the parasitical tendency in some business operations to use some slight variation of already established names as a means of fooling the customer. Names do, of course, have a certain value; but this value is extrinsic to the object or person the names signify, and ultimately the only satisfactory basis of judgment is the one that examines a product or a person for its or his own worth.

SLOGANS AND THEIR USES

Closely related to the psychology of big names is the psychology of the slogan industry, whose aim it is to induce various methods of hidden and sometimes friendly persuasion to get the customer to buy and the voter to vote. The appeal of the slogan industry is directed—through clever and subtle formulas—to what Plato had called the "irrational part" of man, or to what we refer to today as the subconscious. The secret of this mode of appeal lies precisely in the fact that it *is* hidden from consciousness.

From the standpoint of both psychology and logic, the moment we begin to reflect on the slogan, we begin to thwart the advertiser's design and intent. Quite simply he wants us to buy or to vote *on impulse,* and he is concerned to prevent the kind of thinking—both critical and reflective—that logic enjoins us to do. Not, of course, that every impulse is wrong, but that our impulses, too, should be examined to see whether they have any value or not. In our brief study of the fallacy of accent we called special attention to the practice whereby an original statement is distorted by deliberate misplacement of emphasis. As a special instance of this fallacy, the slogan, too, can serve as a method of distracting a person—through misplaced emphasis—from the inherent qualities, or lack of them, of the product he wishes to buy. Suppose an advertising agent wants you to buy an expensive automobile. The last thing he would want to "play up" is the price of the car. Instead he will appeal to your comfort, he will do all that he can to convince you of the superior ride. Or, again, he may appeal to your pride; you in your class or profession deserve nothing but the best, and this brand of car is the best for you, who are no part of the *hoi polloi*. The advertiser will, in fact, utilize everything he knows about the psychology of human attention to get you to think "positively" only about those factors that are calculated to make you respond in some conditioned way.

As to the methods of evoking response, more often than not they involve the clever manipulation of words and pictures combined with the use of psychological laws of association. We have heard much in our society of "guilt by association" but precious little of another factor which is a potent one indeed—of *success* by association, of snob appeal, and in general of the whole social psychology of "keeping up" or competing "with the Joneses." Too, the fallacy of misplaced emphasis has led in our society from the judgment of the superiority of one's own economic class to the judgment of the presumed inferiority in every other respect of all less fortunate classes. The inherent fallacy of the "you deserve" type of advertisement is that it supposes that superfluous goods for the affluent have priority over the necessities of life which the underprivileged lack.

EXERCISE 2.2

A. *Reading Selection.* The following selection from *Time* Magazine highlights some of the points we have made on the use of slogans. In connection with your reading of the article, discuss (1) the value of certain slogans (give examples) and (2) their abuse (give examples).

> In politics, it seems, bad times made good slogans. Herbert Hoover's promise of a "chicken in every pot" did not get him reelected in 1932, but it was a far more ingenious catch phrase than the Republicans' 1944 theme, "Time for a change," or "I like Ike" in 1952. And for all John F. Kennedy's eloquence, no Democratic orator since the Depression has matched Franklin D. Roosevelt's phrasemaking prowess on behalf of the "forgotten man."
>
> To many scholars, all slogans are bad slogans. . . . Indeed, for the majority of voters not inclined to analyze issues for themselves, slogans are a welcome substitute for logical argument. "Most people would rather die than think," said Bertrand Russell. "In fact, some do." Russell's own ban-the-bomb marchers, mindlessly chanting "Better Red than dead," proved his point.
>
> Phrases such as "Peace in our time" . . . invoke "word magic," as linguists call verbal formulas that promise to make dreams come true through sheer force of repetition. . . . The most effective political slogans are timely, yet live long beyond their time. Passing into the language, they help crystallize great issues of the past for future generations: "Give me liberty or give me death"; *"Lebensraum"*; "The world

must be made safe for democracy"; "There'll always be an England"; "unconditional surrender"; "the Great Leap Forward"; "We shall overcome.". . .

The word "slogan," from the Gaelic *sluagh* (army) and *gairm* (a call), originally meant a call to arms—and some of history's most stirring slogans from "Erin go bragh" to "Remember Pearl Harbor" have been just that. . . .

To be fully effective, say psychologists, a slogan should express a single idea in seven words or less. "It is a psychological fact," says Harvard's Gordon Allport, "that seven is the normal limit of rote memory." (Example: telephone numbers.) Whether plugging cat food or a candidate, sloganeers lean heavily on such verbal devices as alliteration ("Korea, Communism, Corruption"), rhyme ("All the way with L.B.J."), or a combination of both ("Tippicanoe and Tyler too"). Other familiar standbys are paradox ("We have nothing to fear but fear itself"), metaphor ("Just the kiss of the hops"), metonymy ("The full dinner pail"), parody (a Norwegian travel folder promises "a Fjord in your Future") and punning ("Every litter bit helps" [sic]). By using what semanticists call "affective" language, many slogans deliberately exploit chauvinism ("Made in Texas by Texans"), xenophobia ("Yankee go home"), insecurity ("Even your best friends won't tell you"), narcissism ("Next to myself I like B.V.D. best"). . . .

English teachers curse Madison Avenue for institutionalizing bad grammar with such calculated lapses as "us Tareyton smokers" and "like a cigarette should." By contrast, some of history's most enduring slogans were plucked from literature. Winston Churchill's call to "blood, sweat and tears"—boiled down from his first statement as Prime Minister in 1940, "I have nothing to offer but blood, toil, tears, and sweat" —was adapted from a passage in a 1931 book by Churchill; but strikingly similar words were used in previous centuries by the British poets John Donne, Byron and Lord Alfred Douglas. [*Time,* October 16, 1964, p. 96] [6]

B. Read Chapter 5, "From Ideal to Image: The Search for Self-Fulfilling Prophesies," in Daniel Boorstin's *The Image,* New York: Harper & Row, 1964, pp. 181–238. Make a two-page report on what you have read, relating it to what you have read in the text.

---

[6] Reprinted by permission. Copyright *Time Inc.* 1964.

chapter 3

Sources of Deceit II

Emotional and Other Types of Appeal

Irrelevance: Its Traditional Forms
Irrelevance: Some Modern Varieties
Assorted Fallacies
Begging the Question
Contradictory Premises

The present chapter is a continuation of our study of nontechnical, informal fallacies. In Chapter 2 the emphasis was on fallacies of language; the weight of this chapter is brought to bear on those fallacies that are psychological in origin—that is, the kind that for the most part contain various sorts of emotional appeal. For reasons of convenience these fallacies are listed under three headings:

1. Irrelevance (ignoring the issue or arguing beside the point, and assorted fallacies)
2. Begging the question
3. Contradictory premises

IRRELEVANCE: Its Traditional Forms

Fallacies of irrelevance (ignoring the issue, arguing beside the point) include any and all those methods of distraction, distortion, omission, or confusion whereby an attempt is made, consciously or unconsciously, to sidetrack attention from the issue at hand.

The bulk of this chapter will consist of an attempt to examine these fallacies and to illustrate their meaning and use. Before we proceed, however, we need to note the intimate connection that exists between them and the psychology of human attention. As is well known, the human mind is extremely limited in its span of attention—in the amount of time it can focus, let us say, on a point of argument or on an issue that needs to be resolved. A strong positive effort at concentration is needed to keep to the point and to wave off the countless distractions that divert the mind from its essential task.

William James, the great American psychologist, tells a very interesting story of himself as a writer. Every time he sat at his desk to do work on a lecture or a book, he continually tricked himself into not doing what he was supposed to do, by sharpening a pencil, filling a pipe or emptying the wastebasket, and so on. The point he means to illustrate is that, given a difficult task, human nature more often than not will look for a method of escape. So too in the matter of logic. Rather than confront an issue that needs to be resolved, we often find ourselves lapsing into some easy method of irrelevance. In fact, we will often go to the extreme of spending more energy in trying to escape a problem than in solving the problem itself. Yet beyond this difficulty of focusing on what is essential, it is a very human trait to avoid unpleasant evidence even when it is patent, and to this end we go out of our way to invent various kinds of evasion.

As a case in hand, let us assume that a person is caught in a traffic violation by a police officer. The policeman asks him whether he knew he went through a red light, and he replies, "Not really, because it was green the last time I saw it." The ambiguity of this statement may lead one to wonder whether the violator suffered a temporary "blackout," whether he simply closed his eyes when the light turned red, or—as is most likely— whether he is trying to ignore the officer's statement. The example in question is in any case a typical method of evasion and may therefore, if it is taken seriously, be regarded as a fallacy of irrelevance.

Fallacies of this sort, if deliberately practiced, are a form of intellectual dishonesty, a none too hidden "source of deceit." The problem, however, is this: in view of the many ways in which the genius of human invention can fabricate, lie, and distort, how shall we provide a list of these fallacies? Though no perfect list is available, the remainder of this chapter will be an attempt to classify some of the leading ways the human mind can "get off the track." As you study these fallacies, however, do not hesitate to add to the list as you see fit.

Ad Hominem

From this point on the reader will encounter various Latin names of fallacies that have become part of the vocabulary of logic. Foremost among them is the "ad hominem" argument. Literally translated, this expression means an appeal "to the man"—in the deprecatory sense of trying to discredit an argument by discrediting the opponent himself. The technique is to show, for example, that So-and-so is unqualified to make a certain kind of statement *because,* let us say, of his background, his prejudices, and so on. It is often characterized by such expressions as "Look who's talking" and "Consider the source."

The "ad hominem" appeal often assumes the form of name calling—a practice that involves the use of labels which are a direct attack on the character of an individual—as a method, let us say, of disqualifying him as a witness in court. In highly emotional situations we often hear such vituperative labels as "thief," "murderer," "good-for-nothing," or whatever epithet might serve to attack the person himself.

A peculiarly modern form of the "ad hominem" type is the fallacy of *psychological reductionism,* or what might alternatively be called the *psychoanalytic* fallacy. This fallacy consists in psychoanalyzing the opponent instead of facing up to his argument. Some of its typical forms are as follows:

1. "No wonder you take the position you do, *because* you are an official of this university."
2. "It's no surprise that you believe in the tenets of Islam. You were brought up that way by your parents."
3. "Your refusal to marry me is irrational. It must go back to some repression you suffered in your early childhood."

The assumption in all three cases is that the opponent is prevented by his position or upbringing or early experiences from thinking for himself or making his own decisions.

Be it noted here that the person who is guilty of this fallacy denies in effect that his opponent is a free and rational agent, and in this sense his technique is an "appeal to the man."

Another variation of the "ad hominem" argument is the method of the "tu quoque" (literally, "you also") statement.

Example: "You accused me of stealing yesterday. Well, didn't you admit that when *you* were a boy, *you too* used to steal your neighbor's apples?"

The technique here is obviously one of irrelevance; it attempts to distract attention from the issue at hand by putting the blame on someone else who is presumed guilty of the same thing. The point to note here is that another person's guilt in no significant way detracts from the first accusation. A further example is the following:

"Officer, I admit I double-parked, but why do you want to give me a ticket? A thousand other people in the city are doing the same thing right now, and you yourself have probably done it too."

One last remark concerning "ad hominem" appeals: there are circumstances in which such an appeal may have a bearing—for example, in a court situation. Frequently witnesses are discredited, and lawfully so, on the grounds either that they are habitual liars or insufficiently informed. In circumstances of this sort it is perfectly legitimate to "consider the source." Further, it is part of critical thinking to be wary of those individuals who set themselves up as authorities in areas where they have little or no knowledge at all. Movie actors may not be the best judges of the education and political needs of the country, nor is it the case that baseball heroes, television ads notwithstanding, are always the best judges of shaving cream.

Appeal to the Mob (Ad Populum)

Leaders of all sorts frequently address themselves in a highly emotional way to the prejudices of their audiences, and this is what is meant by "mob" appeal. In a highly charged, emotional situation people often put aside their powers of critical thinking and allow themselves to be "carried away" by demagogic appeals. The need, then, is to "keep your cool" in situations of this sort.

"Mob appeal" is a source of deceit in various ways, of course. We should note that popular speakers who are passionately pleading a particular cause are seldom given to subtle distinctions. On the contrary, they frequently give a one-sided picture of a situation by distorting or suppressing relevant points of evidence. Too, their appeal is often made to the worst elements in human nature, including racial and national hatred, and at times an audience can be worked up to a point of violence. As against a fair-minded appeal to reason and logic, the orator relying on mob psychology more often than not resorts to prejudice, opposition to the law, disorder, and confusion.

Example: My friends, you know that this man deserves to be hung *without the delay of the law*. Why should anyone who flouts the law be allowed to use that same law in self-defense? I say to you, rouse up your anger against this man, and string him up on that big oaktree. You know better than any old-fogey judge how to handle a criminal like this when you see one. I tell you, give him what he deserves!

Appeal to Fear (Ad Baculum)

In its original meaning the "ad baculum" argument was an appeal to physical force—literally an appeal "to the stick." In modern society, however, the stick can just as well be a machine gun, an army, or even a nuclear bomb. As against any attempt to persuade by rational means, the appeal to fear consists of an endeavor to scare off one's opponent by whatever violent means at one's disposal.

In an era in which psychological methods are as dominant as physical ones, the appeal to fear is often made on a much more subtle basis. An example is the play and subsequent movie in which a villainous husband uses all sorts of devices to persuade an innocent wife that she is going mad, with the threat that if she rebels against his "treatment," he will put her away. Less ingeniously, perhaps, but with the same degree of effectiveness, a worker is often persuaded to "think" the same way as his boss, lest he run the risk of losing his job. Or again, with far less subtlety, a rebellious member of a syndicate is often told that unless he agrees with the group, he may on some fine morning be found at the base of an elevator shaft. One need only examine some of the older detective plays and movies to classify various methods of the appeal to force.

Appeal to Pity (Ad Misericordiam)

A humane spirit requires us to show pity and compassion whenever such responses are appropriate. But the appeal to pity is the attempt to substitute pity for more suitable rational persuasion. The fallacy, therefore, is based on an irrelevant appeal to the sentiment of pity. The following is a somewhat hyperbolic example. A young man is on trial for slaying both of his parents. The defense lawyer addresses himself to the jury: "How can you possibly pronounce sentence on this young man? For one thing, he didn't know what he was doing. But more: if you convict him, the consequences will be too horrible to contemplate. Can you imagine what it would be like to send a poor orphan to prison?"

A further example of exaggerated appeal to pity is typified by the many "heartbreakers" professors are obliged to listen to at the time of final exams. Consciously or otherwise, a hard core of students will consistently excuse their academic deficiencies by sob stories of all sorts. The correlation between uncles' heart attacks and the scheduling of final exams often leads professors to presume that the appeal to pity is in many instances contrived and imaginary rather than objective and real.

Another instance of an unsuited appeal to sentiment is the custom of

70958

soliciting contributions for every conceivable cause. The long-suffering American public in particular is the victim of appeals of this sort.

> *Example:* "In the name of patriotism you must give until it hurts to relieve the misery of people who suffer from arthritis. Support your local arthritis society and relieve the distress of millions of people."

In such a situation, not only is it the case that the appeal to pity is misdirected: appeals of this sort also involve a fallacy of division: because you can support *this* good cause and that, you can support *all* good causes. A further example is the following:

> *Example:* "Look, Joe, all I'm asking—*for old times' sake*—is a little loan of five hundred dollars for a down payment on this beautiful new Chevy. Can you find it in your heart to refuse such a modest request from an old friend?

(This last example also contains the fallacy, described later in the chapter, of *internal inconsistency,* since for most persons a loan of $500 is hardly a "little" one.)

Viewed from yet another angle, the appeal to pity takes an altogether different twist, giving rise to what we might call the "sentimentalist fallacy." This fallacy consists of *feigning pity where none actually exists.* Very often people "weep crocodile tears" in a situation where motives for weeping are unrelated to the actual weeping itself, as when a child sometimes weeps loudly and mournfully in order to get some new toy that he does not actually need. In a very penetrating remark William James once said that the "sentimentalist fallacy" consists in weeping over injustice in the abstract—but combined with the failure to take any action when one meets injustice face to face because the circumstances make action vulgar.

Appeal to Reverence (Ad Verecundiam)

Respect for authority is a good thing, but when "pulling rank" is used to disguise the lack of a rational defense, we have an "appeal to reverence." As a case in point, if a nation is waging a highly dubious war and a substantial number of citizens express protest against that war, it is irrelevant to suggest paternalistically that "the President knows best." Without a doubt the President has at his disposal information not available to the general public, but in fairness to the citizens, it is wrong simply to appeal to presidential authority alone. The question is not whether the President has authority or not, but whether he is using it wisely. In such situations it is incumbent upon the leaders of the country to make clear why they have adopted this policy or that; failing such an explanation, the citizens have every right to be dissatisfied with an appeal to authority alone.

Appeal to Ignorance (Ad Ignorantiam)

In common parlance the appeal to ignorance is often referred to as a "snow job." It is typified by the method of a speaker who attempts to impress his point upon uninformed hearers by citing a variety of statistics which the audience is in no position to analyze or check. Many of our present-day advertisements, too, are striking examples of the so-called appeal to ignorance; products are sold on the basis of unchecked claims that they contain some new chemical formula hitherto unknown to science.

Example: Ladies. and gentlemen, I invite you to buy our new hyper-activated, siliconed, silicated nutranium-carbonated acid. It is an absolutely reliable means of relieving stomach distress because no such combination of chemicals has ever been produced by our competitors. Try our product once, and you will never again switch to another brand.

The appeal to ignorance is often used, in the language of slang, as a means of "faking out" the person you are trying to persuade. Surprisingly enough, many persons—for want of critical thinking—often appear satisfied with an "explanation" that does not really explain.

IRRELEVANCE: Some Modern Varieties

We have just examined some of the traditional types of irrelevant appeal. This list is by no means exhaustive, however, and for this reason the author asks the reader to consider other methods of irrelevance that are part of day-to-day experience.

Appeal to Pride

The appeal to pride, or snob appeal, is a ready source of deceit for persons who are susceptible to it.

Example: Buy this sixteen-cylinder sports car. Someone like you deserves the very best.

Note that the advertiser does not know who "you" are.

Appeal to Shame

The irrelevant appeal to shame consists of an attempt to induce a feeling of guilt where none should exist.

Example: "I'm surprised that you would ever play such a dirty trick as to beat your own father at Ping-Pong. Shame on you."

Fallacy of Idealization

Another instance in which sentiment takes precedence over logic is evidenced by the all too human propensity to romanticize either some past or some possible future event.

Idealization of the Past

Often it is irrelevant to downgrade, let us say, some present situation, event, or value on the grounds that it docs not compare with some romanticized version of past experience. Frequently this fallacy of irrelevance blends with the fallacy of forgetful induction (see Chapter 13), as when a person fails to consider prices in relation to wages.

Example: "Things will never again be the same. I remember the good old days, when your grandfather and I rented an apartment for twenty dollars a month."

EXERCISE 3.1

Discuss elements in a situation similar to the above that are often exaggerated, romanticized, or omitted. Give your own examples.

Appeal to the Future

An irrelevant appeal to the future is made whenever on the basis of a false hope it is assumed that some single event in the future will be the solution to all or most of the problems that are experienced in the present.

Examples:
1. "Once I get married, I'll be rid of the slavery of living with my mother and dad."
2. "Life will be worth living again once I get out of school. No more term papers, grades, part-time jobs, and so on."
3. "There's nothing I'm looking forward to more than the period of

glorious retirement. I'll be able to sleep as late as I want in the morning, and I'll have enough to live on—without working—for the rest of my life."

Argument from Irrelevant Extremes

There is no upper limit to the number of irrelevant appeals human nature can devise in a "tight" situation, and one of the strangest of them all is what this author calls the *appeal to irrelevant extremes*. This argument often consists in an attempt to avoid responsibility or blame on the grounds that the accuser is imposing impossible standards on the person who is being criticized or accused.

Examples:
1. *Mother:* "Johnny, I want you to stop stealing money from my dresser drawer."
   Johnny: "Do you expect me to be a saint?"
2. Professor Wimple accuses a student of using improper references in some of his footnotes.
   Student: "Do you expect me to be the world's greatest scholar? Besides, I resent the implication that I am a liar."
3. Father asks his sixteen-year-old son to move a pile of stones.
   Son: "Do you think, Dad, that I'm another Hercules?"
4. *Bill:* "I maintain that the government should increase its welfare benefits."
   Tom: "On your recommendation, then, the country might just as well go Communist."

Note: It is a perfectly legitimate form of argument to reject an opponent's antecedent if the consequence to which it leads is false, undesirable, absurd, and so forth (see Chapter 12). It is illegitimate, however, to reject an antecedent by appealing to consequences that do not actually follow from it—whether by the method of extremes, as illustrated here, or by any other method. Any such attempt results in a general fallacy of irrelevance.

ASSORTED FALLACIES

Until now we have examined various sources of deceit—most of them based on an emotional appeal that is irrelevant to the issue at hand. However, not every instance of ignoring the issue is based on an emotional appeal, and here we wish to consider a few of the remaining traditional forms.

Fallacy of Accident

In the following chapter the discussion cautions against the practice of judging by appearances alone. In a similar vein we here take up the fallacious habit of judging by "accidental" qualities rather than by those that are essential and to the point. A young man is faced with the decision of choosing a graduate school: since the choice is mainly one of academic excellence, it would be irrelevant and mistaken for him to imagine that the best school is the one with the best parking lots, athletic facilities, and beaches. Should he base his decision mainly or exclusively on these latter factors, he would incur a *fallacy of accident*. The fallacy of accident consists of a judgment or a decision based on some factor or factors that are only incidental to a situation rather than essential to it. More often than not, this fallacy is the result of allowing oneself to be guided by psychological associations rather than by essential and relevant facts.

Examples:
1. A young lady wishes to marry a young man because he is a "superb" dancer. She commits a fallacy of accident if she fails to consider other factors that are of more fundamental importance, such as those relating to whether he will be a good husband and father.
2. A young man decides to buy a car because it has two side-view mirrors and a double muffler. His main concern should be with the quality of the car's performance.
3. A young man greatly admires a certain professor who has a beard and smokes a pipe. The young man, wishing to become a professor, grows a beard and takes up pipe smoking. He is guilty of a fallacy of accident if he in any way supposes that the accidental qualities of wearing a beard and smoking a pipe will make him a good professor.

False Analogy

The use of analogy is valid when the point of comparison—upon which the analogy rests—is to the point. We have an argument, however, from false analogy whenever relevant points of difference are ignored.

Example: "You ride your bike to school. What was good enough for your grandfather should be good enough for you."

The relevant point of difference is that when grandfather rode a bicycle to school, he did not have to face today's heavy traffic.

The fallacy of false analogy is also interpreted as follows: a person assumes mistakingly that, because two persons, events, or objects are similar in one respect, they must be similar in other respects also.

Example: Maimonides and Aquinas were both medieval scholars who developed philosophical proofs for the existence of God. Therefore, they were both Christians.

As a matter of fact, one of them was a Jew, the other a Christian. The fact that they used similar arguments does not make them similar in every *other* respect. (This fallacy, incidentally, is in some instances equivalent to the fallacy of the undistributed middle.)

Special Case

The fallacy of the special case consists in arguing that what is true of one or more special cases is true of all cases without exception. It is assumed, for example, that because in some cases the use of alcoholic liquor leads to ruin, therefore all use of alcoholic liquor is wrong (that is, for everybody); that because in some instances almsgiving is conducive to indolence, therefore almsgiving should in all instances be discouraged; that because in some cases a medicine prevents patients from coughing, therefore it should be prescribed for all patients regardless of the nature or cause of their cough.

In general, any unwarranted "leap" from the truth of the particular to the supposed truth of the universal is an instance of the fallacy of special case. Two of the commonest forms of this fallacy are concluding from the abuse of a thing in a few particular cases to its complete abolition and concluding from the effectiveness of a certain remedy in a few cases to its effectiveness for all similar cases without exception.

Note: The fallacy of special case may certainly be regarded as an inductive fallacy; it is mentioned here because it is also a fallacy of irrelevance: the special case is irrelevant to the general rule. For example, it may be true in an emergency situation that people can and will work for as long as twenty hours a day; however, it is false to assume that a twenty-hour workday should be prescribed as a normal workload.

Dicto Simpliciter

To have meaning and relevance generalized statements often need to be qualified or "toned down." The failure to take this factor into account leads to a fallacy called *dicto simpliciter*. What this fallacy means, then, is the attempt to reason from an unqualified statement to a particular instance to which it does not apply.

Examples:
1. Youth is inexperienced. Since Bill is a youth, he must be inexperienced.
   Remark: Youth need not be inexperienced in every respect. The inference does not follow that Bill is unqualifiedly inexperienced.
2. Damp climates are not conducive to health. Since this climate is damp, it is therefore not conducive to health.
   Remark: The need to qualify is again apparent, since someone with a certain type of skin problem, for example, may find a damp climate to be the only kind that agrees with him.

Hypothesis Contrary to Fact

The fallacy of hypothesis contrary to fact supposes that some event would have taken place *if* another which did not take place had been fulfilled. The fallacy is one of irrelevance precisely because there is no way of knowing the consequences of an unfulfilled hypothetical event.

Examples:
1. Jim to his wife: "If I had not married you, I would have remained single, in which case I would have retained my freedom to go bowling every Saturday night with the boys."
   Remark: The fallacy of omission or irrelevance here is Jim's failure to consider, among other things, that he might have married someone else.
2. If you had elected *our* man to the presidency, the country would not be in the mess that it is in right now."
   Remark: Perhaps not, but, on the other hand, it might be in a "worse mess" than it is now. There simply is no way of knowing— one way or the other.

Hypothesis contrary to fact assumes a kind of knowledge we do not have, and the person who is guilty of its use is like the "Monday-morning quarterback," who knows how to call the plays once the contingencies of a situation have been removed. It is precisely the contingencies of a situation that make that situation doubtful.

BEGGING THE QUESTION

Enough has been said of those fallacies that ignore issues (*ignoratio elenchi*) or argue beside the point (*praster rem*). Now a word is in order about the fallacy of *begging the issue* or the question at hand (*petitio principii*). By this fallacy is meant any attempt to assume as proved the very point that is to be established. This can happen in a number of ways, and one of them is by the use of synonyms: "The color of your eyes is a hereditary factor because it is a characteristic handed down to you by your parents." The question still remains: what proof is there for the assertion?

The Vicious Circle, or Arguing in a Circle

A common form of this fallacy is the familiar vicious circle. A circular argument takes places when a person gives a reason for some proposition that he maintains (his conclusion) and proceeds forthwith (as a means of defending the reason he has invoked) to prove it by means of the conclusion.

> *Example:* All radicals should be deported from our country because they are a constant menace to good government. These men are a constant menace to good government because they are radicals.

Complex Questions

Another instance of begging the issue is the fallacy of *complex question*—formulating a question in such a way as to leave no real choice for the respondent. In most instances a simple "yes" or "no" involves an admission that the respondent is unwilling to make.

> *Examples:*
> 1. "How long have you been embezzling funds from the bank?"
> 2. "Have you kept your resolution of not smoking three packs of cigarettes a day?"

The answer to a question of this sort lies in a denial of the double supposition upon which it rests.

Suppose, for instance, that some aggressive salesman asks, "Have you placed an order yet for your new refrigerator?" I might promptly reply that neither did I place an order for a refrigerator nor do I consider it mine until I buy it (unless, of course, he chooses to give it away).

Question-Begging Epithets

Also to be classed under the fallacy of begging the question is the question-begging epithet—one that very compactly either commends its object to the listener (or reader) or equally compactly condemns it.

Examples:

the fair-play amendment	the century of enlightenment
the people's candidate	the Dark Ages
the favorite of millions	a do-nothing Congress

CONTRADICTORY PREMISES

As a final note to our study of fallacies we must examine the *fallacy of internal inconsistency* or *contradictory premises*. This fallacy occurs when someone contradicts himself within the course of a single statement or an argument.

Examples:
1. *Professor:* Young man, I saw you copying from your neighbor.
   Student: Prof, I wasn't copying, I was just looking at Bill's answers to get some fresh ideas for my own.
   Remark. The internal inconsistency of this statement lies in the attempt to make a distinction without a difference.
2. There is one and only one remedy for people who believe in panaceas: to study logic.
   Remark. Apparently it did not occur to the person who made this statement that he himself is prescribing a panacea.
3. This vacuum cleaner is absolutely and unconditionally guaranteed except for parts and labor.
   Remark. Caveat emptor!

EXERCISE 3.2

A. Attempt as best you can to analyze the fallacies present in the following examples:

1. I cannot agree with the political philosophy of a man who twenty-five years ago was hauled into court on a charge of drunken driving. What kind of an example is that for our youth?
2. Vote for me, and not for a political party, because I am the people's candidate, the candidate of your choice in the next election.

3. "All of us are equal, but some of us are more equal than others." (Pig's statement, in *Animal Farm* by George Orwell)

4. Ever since I've met you I've had all sorts of bad luck.

5. "It is a Freudian dogma that no one is capable of judging the validity of the theory until he has been successfully analyzed. Since no one is classified as having completed his analysis until he has accepted the theory, apparently only those in agreement are regarded as competent to comment." (From "Some Reflections on Psychoanalysis, Hypnosis, and Faith Healing" by C. H. Tigpen and H. M. Cleckley, in *The Conditioning Therapies,* New York: Holt, Rinehart, and Winston, Inc., 1964, p. 100.) To which fallacy were the authors calling attention?

6. "Buying a new car helps spread the wealth, and therefore is patriotic. You don't want to be an unpatriotic hoarding slob, do you?" (From an intentionally humorous ad by a local credit union.)

7. The federal government has no right to investigate the financial affairs of a private citizen, because a citizen's private affairs are none of the government's business.

8. I don't agree with people who believe in panaceas, so in my thinking there is only one remedy for this type of a person: make him take a solid course in logic.

9. "Carefully dressed students make higher grades. A recent survey of students discloses that 'those who are carefully and neatly dressed have much higher grade averages than those who are not.' Well, we're not psychologists or logicians, but we certainly can help solve this problem. For that well-groomed look, all you have to do is get all your soiled and rumpled clothes together and call us." (From an advertisement for a cleaning business.)

10. A local newspaper prints a "weekly progress report" of community developments. The following item appeared under "Progress." "CRIME: First quarter report shows City losing battle as crime increases 47 percent over first three months."

B. Identify the fallacies contained in the following dialogue.

BUYING A CAR

Salesman: Good morning, sir. May I help you?

Buyer: Yes, thank you. My wife and I have decided it is time to trade in our two-year-old car for a new one. I understand that this is a good time of the year to trade.

Salesman: Yes sir. Your old car is worth much more now than it will be later on this year. We will give you so much on trade-in value that you would be foolish not to trade and save money. Now what would you like to get? A wagon? A nice coupe? A sedan? Or maybe the new sports model?

Buyer: We'd like to look around for a while.

Salesman: Okay. Here is our new station wagon. This car has plenty of luggage space, lots of leg room, four extra-wide doors and a two-way tailgate. And just look at those seats! Children can't damage those seats; they are made of foam rubber covered with hexoplastilene, a new miracle fiber developed by the makers of the car.

Wife: Well, we don't have children, and we really were looking for something a little smaller.

Salesman: I have just what you want. This is our deluxe sedan, fully equipped for your comfort. Kick those tires—go ahead, kick them. Those are the best tires on the road today. They are made by the same company that makes Snappy Stretch girdles, and you know how good they are! Well, your wife would, sir.

Wife: Does this model have air conditioning?

Salesman: This car has tinted glass all around, blocking out those heat rays and leaving you in cool comfort. And let me show you the new, enlarged air vents. You always have cool, fresh air in this car.

Buyer: How is it on gas?

Salesman: Sir, you will never run out of gas in this car. When your tank gets low, this little red light comes on, reminding you to get gas, and it lets you know that you still have three gallons of gas left in the tank. How about that?

Wife: Now I think that is very practical. No one with any sense at all would ever run out of gas. How much is this car?

Salesman: We are letting this one go for a mere five thousand dollars—but that's for today only.

Buyer: Well . . . I really don't care for the color of this one. Could we see something else?

Salesman: Over here we have the economy model of this same car, but I want to point out that this is still a quality car. Just try those seats. You'll think you're sitting in your favorite easy chair. These seats are the same as the seats in the deluxe model, so you know that they will ride nice and smooth.

Buyer: I haven't seen too many of these around. Aren't they any good?

Salesman: This model sold over fifty thousand two years ago, and that many people couldn't be wrong.

Buyer: Well, I don't know. I was talking to Jack Klug at Klug's Garage, and he said that these cars were not made too well. He said that the block is weak and the body rusts out quickly.

Salesman: Jack Klug, hmph! Did you know that he's been married three times, was arrested for reckless driving, and once filed bankruptcy on another garage he operated? What does he know about cars?

Wife: I agree. What right does he have to talk like that? Anyone who has been married three times can't be very trustworthy.

Buyer: Anyway, this isn't quite what I wanted. Maybe something a little sportier.

Salesman: Yes, sir. We have two sports models. This little sports job is as good a car as you'll find on any lot. It has adjustable seats, roll-up windows, a radio, and a heater.

Wife: How dependable is this car?

Salesman: Leadfoot Louie, the famous racing driver, has one of these, and if anyone knows cars, he does.

Buyer: What's the engine like?

Salesman: This car has an air-cooled engine that runs with maximum efficiency in both cold and hot climates, and besides that, it never needs water or anti-freeze.

Buyer: It seems awfully small to me. There is no back seat, so we wouldn't be able to take friends with us any place.

Salesman: All right, step right over here. This is our grand sports model, with all the optional equipment installed to save you money. If you buy all this equipment separately, you'll be paying both for the car and for the equipment. By buying all the options with the car, you'll just be paying the one low price. You can't beat that, can you?

Wife: I don't know too much about foreign-made cars. Is this one well built?

Salesman: Lady, this car is made in a factory in England just down the road from the Rolls Royce factory. I'm sure you have heard of that car, haven't you?

Wife: Oh, yes; they are very expensive, so they must be good.

Buyer: I'd like to take it for a test drive, if you don't mind.

Salesman: Certainly, I'll get the key. I can tell that it would be useless to try to fool you. Anyone who wants to test-drive a car really knows what he is doing.

(Later—in the car)

Salesman: I can tell that you've driven a sports car before, sir. Where did you get your experience?

Buyer: I never actually owned a sports car, but I used to race Go-Karts, so I know a lot about driving competition cars. Do you think my wife will be able to learn to drive this car?

Salesman: Oh, sure. According to national statistics, women are better drivers than men, so she won't have any trouble at all.

Wife: Is this car as economical as those little German-made bugs?

Salesman: This car is as economical as any other car in its class.

Buyer: I like this car, but I also drove a new Whizbang Mark IV, and I really——

Salesman: No one in his right mind and with any knowledge of cars at all would buy a Whizbang. When did you get the silly notion of getting one?

Buyer: Well, I . . . uh, I really didn't intend to get one. I just tried one out because a friend asked me to. He doesn't know too much about cars, though.

Wife: I've seen a lot of young people and teenagers driving this model lately. Is it supposed to appeal to the younger set rather than mature people, who are a little older?

Salesman: We've sold several of these to teenagers, but I'd like to see more adult drivers in these cars. Those teenagers are giving the car a bad name. Why, just last week I sold one of these to a teenager in college, and he didn't get two blocks from the lot before he had an accident. Teenagers are bad drivers—just look at his example.

(Back at the car lot)

Buyer: Well, I really like the car, and my wife seems to enjoy it too, but I'm not sure we can afford it yet.

Salesman: Anyone can afford a car at this lot, sir. Just step inside, and we'll show you what real friends we can be. That idea of losing your shirt when you trade cars just doesn't apply here like it does when you trade with other car lots. Now, what was your name again?

C. Carefully examine the following interview for the fallacies it contains. Some of the fallacies are indicated by number, and the answers are provided at the end of the selection. Before you look up the answers, try to identify the fallacies for yourself. Keep in mind that there is often room for disagreement over fallacies and that sometimes a single example combines more than one fallacy at a time.

ALL IN A DAY'S WORK

The conversation below takes place in the office of a marriage counselor who is employed by a state-supported agency. In response to a request for help from Mr. and Mrs. Homer Sapiens, the counselor has made an appointment to meet with them at this hour. Introductions have been made, and all are seated, waiting for someone to launch the painful topic. The characters are:

C. . . . . *Marriage Counselor*
Mr. . . . . *Mr. Homer Sapiens*
Mrs. . . . . *Mrs. Homer Sapiens*

C.: Well, folks, what seems to be the problem?

Mrs.: We think we ought to get a divorce.

C.: Why?

Mrs.: Because we aren't happy together. We are bound to be happier apart.

C.: What is causing all the unhappiness? After all, every cloud has a silver lining. (1)

Mrs.: He stops by the bar on his way home every Friday and drinks and gambles and spends money foolishly. After I work so hard [sobbing] to keep expenses down and to increase our savings, (2) he wastes the money in that tavern.

C.: Mr. Sapiens, how long have you been squandering the family income in this manner? (3)

Mr.: Now, just a minute. It's always been the custom in my family for the men to spend the money as they see fit. (4) I give her plenty to take care of household expenses. Besides, she wastes money having that silly poodle groomed. (5) I can sure have a drink and a hand of cards if I want.

Mrs.: That's the way men reason. (6) My sister's husband used to stop at the bar for just one quick drink. It wasn't long before he was gambling away all their money. He got thrown into jail for fighting and lost his job because of it. (7)

Mr.: Well, I'm not your sister's husband. Besides, I don't blame him for drinking. She couldn't even put a decent meal on the table. (8)

C.: Folks, if I could just inject some thoughts here——

Mr.: Besides, her liberal-minded mother (9) is always interfering with the way I discipline Junior.

C.: Why do you say she is liberal-minded?

Mr.: Because she believes in being liberal with the kids. (10)

Mrs.: Don't you criticize my mother. She sacrificed and worked so hard to bring up eight fine children, who all turned out to be upstanding citizens in the community; she certainly knows what is best for children—and that includes Junior. (11)

Mr.: I suppose you are the shining example of how well your mother's methods work! (12) It doesn't matter, anyway. A father and son understand each other better because they are both men. It's up to me to decide how to discipline Junior.

Mrs.: Well, Junior's music teacher did not agree with you. (13) She said *we* should discipline Junior.

Mr.: What she said was that we should *discipline* Junior, (14) because she felt that "discipline" was what Junior had not been getting.

C.: Folks, it appears that we——

Mrs.: Besides, *McCall's Magazine* says——(15)

Mr.: What does *McCall's Magazine* have to do with how I bring up my kid? [Turning to Counselor] This boy has stayed out until four A.M. for three nights now, when he was instructed to be home by midnight.

Mrs.: But he was out with a lovely girl, the daughter of one of the old, established families of the community. (16) Junior just needs understanding.

Mr.: I understand him, all right. (17) That's why I insist on disciplining him now. I suppose you would have me set him up in his own apartment and provide him with a car of his own! (18)

C.: Folks, I insist on having a word here. Now, Mr. and Mrs. Sapiens, I am sure that you are anxious for Junior to be provided with a proper environment for his development. We must try to find a solution to your problem, because the state is also concerned about Junior. Many children are removed from their homes and parents each year, you know, because the state feels that they are not growing up in a wholesome atmosphere. Now, some boys with Junior's disciplinary problems respond very well to a military-school program. Some of them even go on to become high-ranking officers in the military service. Therefore, I think a couple of years at a good military school is just what we need here. It did wonders for my cousin's boys. (19)

Mr.: What are you trying to suggest? Why, no Sapiens ever needed to be sent to a correctional institution in all the history of my family. And no Sapiens has ever failed to be a solid citizen of his community and provide well for his family and be a good father to his children. Junior will turn out all right, too. (20)

Mrs.: Why are you trying to make a professional soldier out of my son? (21) The Sapienses have been cattlemen for generations. [Turning to Mr. Sapiens] That's an insult to your family, Homer!

Mr.: I'll say!

  C.: But, folks, that's not what I said at all. Your family tradition is not what I meant to insult. (22) I mean——

Mr.: Just you never mind. We'll raise our boy like we see fit. You people are always giving advice where it's not wanted. (23) I always thought you marriage counselors knew more about raising children than I do, but I can see now that all you sociologists are incompetents. (24) Come on, honey, we have to be heading home.

Mrs.: Yes, dear. Good day, Counselor.

(Several minutes later, Counselor speaks into his intercom.)

  C.: Miss Jones, would you please bring in my bottle of tranquilizers— and get my psychiatrist on the phone.

ANSWERS: LIST OF FALLACIES

1. False analogy (arguing from a metaphor).
2. Appeal to pity.
3. Complex question.
4. Appeal to reverence.
5. Appeal to the man (tu quoque).
6. Appeal to the man.
7. Special case.
8. Appeal to the man (abuse).
9. Question begging (question-begging epithet).
10. Question begging (vicious circle).
11. Appeal to reverence, appeal to unsuitable authority, appeal to pity, special case.
12. Appeal to the man (abuse).
13. Appeal to unsuitable authority.
14. Accent.
15. Appeal to unsuitable authority.
16. Appeal to reverence.
17. Accent.
18. Fallacy of irrelevant extremes (false cause).
19. Special case.
20. Dicto simpliciter.
21. Irrelevant extremes.
22. Amphiboly.
23. Internal inconsistency (they wouldn't be in the presence of the counselor if they were not seeking his advice).
24. Ad hominem.

chapter 4

Judgments and the Making of Decisions

Categorical Judgments; Truth and Falsity
Critical Thinking
The Art of Making Decisions
Proposition Defined: The Categorical Proposition

Having acquired some grasp both of the way logic and language relate to each other and of the various types of emotional appeal, we can now move on to a study of judgments, and in particular to the categorical judgment. Our study of judgments in this chapter will be related to the important matter of critical thinking and the logic of making decisions.

CATEGORICAL JUDGMENTS; TRUTH AND FALSITY

What does the mind do when it judges? To keep matters simple, we shall confine ourselves here to judgment in one of its most primary and basic senses—that is, the *categorical* judgment. Every categorical judgment consists of an assertion or denial that involves two distinct objects of thought. We must first have something about which to judge, such as "microscope," and then we must affirm or deny some predicate of that subject. The judgment itself takes place when we actually affirm or deny that an attribute does or does not belong to this subject. Thus I am judging when I assert of this microscope that it is "suited for purposes of scientific observation" or that it is "not to be treated as a toy." [1]

Keeping in mind these considerations, we may accordingly define a

---

[1] Judgment is not a mere association of images, whether sensory or conceptual. To judge is not merely to place in juxtaposition two objects of thought, so that first one ("this play") is thought of and immediately thereafter the other ("hailed by the critics as a great success"). In judging, the mind does not act as a slide projector, as it were, which involves the use of successive movements to create a unified effect. On the contrary, the mind is active, not passive. It unites or disunites two objects of thought in a single act, and simultaneously affirms or denies accordingly.

categorical judgment as an act according to which *the mind asserts one object of thought to agree or disagree with another*. We can thus say that the prerequisites of judgment—its subject and predicate—are its matter, whereas the assertion of agreement or disagreement constitutes its form.

Truth and Falsity

It is beyond the scope of logic to determine the various means of testing the truth of judgments—that is, of establishing the various criteria of truth. Yet, for purposes of logic, it is important to know that *a judgment is true* if it affirms of its subject an attribute that really belongs to it (for example, "Canada is a North American country") or if it denies of its subject an attribute that the subject does not possess (for example, "Detroit is not the capital of the United States").

On the other hand, *a judgment is false* if it affirms of its subject an attribute that does not belong to the subject (for example, "France is an Asiatic nation") or if it denies of its subject an attribute that the subject really possesses (for example, "Alabama is not a southern state").

CRITICAL THINKING

Technical considerations as to the meaning of categorical judgments lead us to examine some practical aspects concerning the making of *any* judgments. For one thing, though making a judgment involves more than mere association of images, many persons nevertheless fail to base their judgments on anything else. Guided as they are by impulse, by attractive images that flash across their minds, they formulate their judgments without sufficient consideration of the evidence at hand and often make unwise decisions.

Consider, then, that the making of a judgment in the fullest sense of the word is a kind of measuring process in which the evidence is weighed and carefully examined prior to the making of a decision. It is this process that constitutes "critical" thinking in contrast to thinking as an unreflective act.[2] Here the word "critical" does not mean "picayune," "negative," "cranky," or the like, but applies to the kind of thinking that involves discrimination, reflection, and a conscious awareness of the kind of judgment one is making. As a matter of fact, "critical" derives from the Greek word "critein," which means to judge, to sort out, to distinguish.

In this same connection, we are often told not to judge by appearances, though in a sense there is no other basis for judgment. Perhaps this paradox

---

[2] There is reason to doubt that thinking without reflection is thinking at all. Frequently we tell a person who failed to reflect that he did not *think*.

can be resolved by suggesting that reliance on appearances *alone* is hazardous; this is the error perpetrated by the chronic victim of sensational advertised bargains. On the other hand, all judgment *begins* with appearances. We judge people, for example, by the way they dress, talk, laugh, work, and so on. However, at a certain point it is important to get beyond the appearances, through the proper use of our faculty of judgment and reflection. Quite often a person who consistently frowns turns out to have an unpleasant disposition, but not always. Quite often the book that is attractively written turns out to have meaning and depth, but not always. Quite often the difficult school subject turns out to be the one that is most boring, but not always. In all such instances it is a crucial part of critical thinking not to allow ourselves to be misled by appearances alone and to withhold judgment until we have examined the evidence at hand. From a human point of view it is difficult to postpone judgments, however. The philosopher John Dewey in *The Quest for Certainty* convincingly shows that people will often demand certainty where none is to be found.

To sum up this discussion, let us note that logic demands of us, no matter how informally, that we learn how to judge. Unfortunately, there are few hard-and-fast rules. Critical thinking must be

1. open to evidence;
2. based on a careful consideration of the alternatives involved; and
3. realistically geared to the needs of the situation at hand.

On this last point, where a practical decision is called for, it is often needful to make a judgment on the basis of probabilities where no certainty is to be had.

THE ART OF MAKING DECISIONS

We have already discussed some procedures for making sound practical judgments. Decision making is no easy process, and most people are involved in the making of decisions until the day they die. Though logic has no universal rules for making decisions, the following practical norms should prove of some value to the reader.

1. BRING YOUR MIND TO FOCUS ON THE PROBLEM AT HAND. Think in specific rather than in vague general terms.

2. TAKE SUFFICIENT TIME FOR DELIBERATION. You should not act on impulse; whenever possible, you should consider alternative courses of action.

3. IF HELP IS NEEDED, CONSULT OTHERS, ESPECIALLY THOSE WHO ARE BEST IN A POSITION TO KNOW.

4. EXAMINE THE PROBABLE CONSEQUENCES OF THE ALTERNATIVE YOU ARE PREPARED TO ACCEPT. To the extent possible, you should try to foresee both the short-range and the long-range consequences of a proposed course of action.

5. ACT WHEN THE TIME IS RIPE.

6. HAVING MADE YOUR DECISION DON'T ATTEMPT TO REVERSE IT UNLESS THERE ARE STRONG AND COMPELLING REASONS FOR CHANGE.

EXERCISE 4.1

A. Call to mind some important personal decision you have made in the past. Analyze various factors that were present in the making of your decision (for example, choice of a college or a marriage partner, a business investment, a change of jobs).

B. In the light of what you have read in this and the previous chapter, critically evaluate the following examples.

1. This box of candy must be a superior product. It has a big brand name and it was made in the U.S.A.
2. Look at the guilty look in this man's eye. He must be the one the police are looking for.
3. The girl in the corner of the room has been yawning all afternoon. She must be bored stiff with the lecture.

PROPOSITION DEFINED: THE CATEGORICAL PROPOSITION

For all practical intents we may define a proposition as a sentence that expresses something true or false. On the basis of this statement we can distinguish a propositional sentence from every other kind, such as the following:

1. A sentence expressing a question ("Where are you going?").
2. A sentence expressing a prayer, wish, or hope ("If only I could remember what I said").
3. A sentence expressing an exhortation or a command ("Do this!").
4. A performative sentence—one which functions as an activity ("I

do" in a marriage ceremony; "I baptize you" in a baptismal ceremony).

5. A sentence expressing an exclamation ("Help!").

Most sentences, of course, have meaning, but only those sentences that are characterized as true or false are propositions.

Since the next chapter deals with categorical statements, we may describe this type of statement as one that simply asserts as a matter of fact that

> *a certain predicate does or does not belong to a*
> *given subject,*

such as "The spacecraft is now in orbit" or "Our astronaut is not yet on the moon." The *matter* of a categorical statement consists of its subject and predicate terms, which we shall refer to simply as the S and P terms. Its *form* is the *copula,* which is expressed by the verb *to be* in the present tense:

am	am not
is	is not
are	are not

For purposes of logic it is often advisable to incorporate what is signified by the grammatical verb (if it is other than the verb *to be*) into the predicate term:

> My brother plays football.
> My brother is a football player.

EXERCISE 4.2

A. Tell whether the following are propositions or not.

1. Who's afraid of the big bad wolf?
2. Never mind.
3. Nobody gives a darn.
4. The race is not to the swift alone.
5. Go fly a kite!
6. Easy come, easy go.
7. Everybody join in the singing!

B. Put the following in a logical form.

   1. Good men deserve praise.
   2. Most wives work hard.
   3. Some people swim for a living.

     To sum up what we have said as to the matter and form of categorical judgments and propositions, note carefully Chart 4.1.

Chart 4.1

	Matter	Form
Judgment	Two objects of thought	Mental assertion of agreement or disagreement
Proposition	Subject and predicate terms	Copula

Categorical Statements

In many circles it is a constant comment that *people do not know how to read*. In fact, students are all too familiar with this complaint as it is directed to them by their professors. What is usually meant, of course, is not that people (and students in particular) are complete illiterates, but that they are often poor readers. Whatever the source of this attitude, it should be stated here that one of the best remedies for poor reading habits is a good course in logic, and in particular that part of it which centers on the analysis of propositions.

The present chapter is a study of the most fundamental type, namely, the *categorical statement*. The importance of this chapter can hardly be overstressed—not only for the purpose of good reading habits, but from the more basic point of view of logic itself: unless we can analyze and classify propositions, it is impossible to have an accurate understanding of syllogistic reasoning. Without exaggeration, then, it can be said that the present chapter is the key to much of what follows.

Note: In this chapter, when reference is made simply to *propositions,* it should be understood that we are confining our attention to *categoricals*. The other types will be examined later in the text.

THE QUANTITY OF PROPOSITIONS

The key rule for determining the quantity of single (atomic) categorical statements is formulated in this statement:

> *The quantity of the subject term decides the quantity of the statement as a whole.*

In other words, if you want to know whether your statement is universal, particular, or singular, take a close look at the subject term to see whether it is applied to an entire class (to *all* the members), to only part of the class (some), or to only one member. Thus:

1. universal subject   universal proposition
2. particular subject   particular proposition
3. singular subject   singular proposition

The above may be illustrated as follows:

1. *All* chairs are for sitting.
2. *Some* chairs are maple.
3. *This* chair is an antique.

For purposes of easy handling, singular propositions in logic are usually treated as though they were universal. The classes of statements are therefore reduced to two: universal and particular. Since many propositions, however, have no definite or indicated sign of quantity (all, each, some, few, and so on), we must learn how to classify what logicians call *indesignate propositions*. Note that an indesignate (unspecified) proposition is not an additional class or type of statement that exists alongside one that is universal or particular. Rather, it is a type of statement that must itself be ultimately classified as universal or particular. Thus when we read, "Parents have a responsibility to their children," we should decide for ourselves whether this statement applies to the whole or to only part of the class of parents.

As a method of resolving the doubt, use this rather basic criterion:

> *If the predicate refers to the nature of the subject as such, consider the statement to be universal; otherwise, classify it as particular.*

With reference to the above example ("Parents . . ."), we have a clear-cut instance of a universal statement. Not so in the example "Parents are hard to get along with." Even though a disgruntled adolescent may intend this statement as a generalization, a more objective analysis requires us to restrict it to only part of the class.

There is one other point to consider. Statements beginning with an infinitive or a gerund are generally to be taken as universal statements. Since logically (not merely grammatically) you can't "split" an infinitive, the subject should be taken as an integral unit, and therefore as a class by itself.

THE QUALITY OF PROPOSITIONS

The verb or "copula" of a statement determines in each case what its "quality" is—that is, whether it is an affirmative or a negative statement. Thus all the statements in Column A are affirmative and those in Column B are negative:

A	B
S is P	S is not P
Non-S is P	Non-S is not P
S is non-P	S is not non-P
Non-S is non-P	Non-S is not non-P

Note: A negative term (non-S, non-P) does not make a proposition negative, but a negative copula (verb) does.

QUANTITY AND QUALITY COMBINED

In logic we combine the quantity and quality of categorical statements in such a way as to formulate four basic types: **A, E, I, O.** From now on all categorical statements will have to be categorized in this fashion:

A universal affirmative (All bees are winged.)
E universal negative (No egg is square.)
I particular affirmative (Some holes are dangerous.)
O particular negative (Some cars are not cheap.)

Note that in the **E** proposition, although the copula may *appear* to be affirmative ("No S is P"), it is really negative because of the negative force of the word *no* or *none*. Thus, although the word "no" is prefixed to the subject term, it signifies not only universal quantity, but negative quality as well. To express an **E** proposition one should, accordingly, avoid the defective form: "No S is *not P*." The *not* here is superfluous and should be eliminated.

THE QUANTITY OF THE PREDICATE TERM

In every proposition we can distinguish three traits: the quantity of the subject term, the quantity of the proposition itself (as determined by the quantity of *S*), and the quantity of the predicate term.

Language seldom permits us to affix a sign of quantity to the predicate term. For example, we never say, "All men are *some* mortals." However, we should not think for this reason that the predicate has no extension. Every predicate term does have quantity or extension (universal or particular), and it is just as important to know the quantity of the predicate as that of the subject. The rules for determining the quantity of the predicate are simple:

> 1. *The predicate term of an affirmative proposition* (**A** *or* **I**) *is always to be taken as particular (undistributed).*
> 2. *The predicate term of a negative proposition* (**E** *or* **O**) *is always universal (distributed).*

The practical importance of these two rules in their bearing on the categorical syllogism cannot be overstressed.

The reason for these rules will become clear as we proceed to explain how in each of the four types of propositions *S* and *P* are related to each other *from the standpoint of their extension.*

VENN DIAGRAMS

Categorical propositions can be represented by means of Venn Diagrams. The effectiveness of these diagrams (named after the English logician John Venn) depends on the fact that there are classes of things and that we can speak about certain relationships that exist between these classes. The abstract representation of a class is clearly seen in Diagram 5.1. As yet this diagram is not a proposition, for it says nothing about the

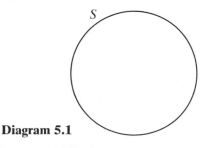

Diagram 5.1

members of the class—it neither affirms nor denies their existence but simply represents a class in general. The two simplest propositions that we can utter are that the class has members or that it does not have members. We can represent these two propositions respectively as shown in Diagram 5.2. The first of these propositions states that the class S has members, and

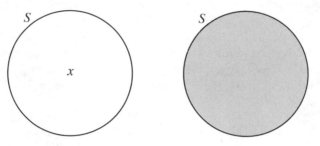

Diagram 5.2

we represent the existence of its members by placing an "x" inside the circle. The second proposition says that there are no members, and this statement is represented by shading inside the circle.

To diagram any categorical proposition, two overlapping circles are required. The subject term is represented by circle S and the predicate by circle P. The general representation of two classes in terms of subject and predicate is given by Diagram 5.3. The first section represents all those

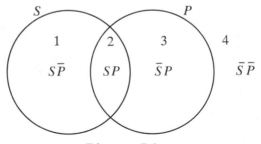

Diagram 5.3

S's which are not P's. The second section represents all those S's which are P's. The third section represents all those P's which are not S's. The section outside of both circles represents all those things which are neither S's nor P's. A tilde ($\sim$) on top of any letter stands for "non." Thus, if S is any class, then $\tilde{S}$ is its contradictory. For example, if S is the class of all Gila monsters, then $\tilde{S}$ is the class of all those things which are non-Gila monsters. In Diagram 5.3 the first section can be represented as $S\tilde{P}$, the second section as SP, the third section as $\tilde{S}P$, and the last section as $\tilde{S}\tilde{P}$. Thus far, the overlapping circles represent abstractly certain sections of two over-lapping classes. No proposition has yet been diagrammed.

Suppose that we want to illustrate the proposition "Some satellites are man-made" by means of Venn diagrams. Letting S represent "satellites" and M represent "man-made," we can diagram the proposition as shown in Diagram 5.4. The class *S* contains only satellites, nothing more and noth-

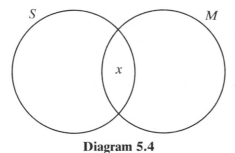

Diagram 5.4

ing less. The class *M* consists of all those things which are man-made, in-cluding hammers, violins, shoes, and so on. But the place where they intersect is made up of *at least one* satellite which is man-made. Our dia-gram says no more and no less than that *some* satellites are man-made—and "some" means at least one. We place an x in the appropriate place to represent that at least one man-made satellite exists.

Any one of the four categorical propositions can be represented by means of Venn diagrams. Thus the proposition "All satellites are man-made" can be expressed by Diagram 5.5. We shade out the left section

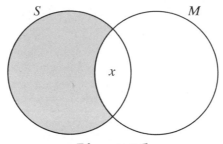

Diagram 5.5

of the overlapping circles to show that there are no satellites which are *not* also man-made; the "x" shows that the class of objects in question exists.

Relative to the correct placement of the "x," note that the truth value of categorical statements depends on the existence of things to which the proposition is applied—with the result that if no such class of objects exists, then the proposition is neither true nor false. Suppose for example, that someone utters the proposition, "All parolians are purple"; since there are no parolians, we can hardly say that the proposition is "false." All we can do in such a case is to show that the intended class of objects simply *does not exist*. Accordingly, in the examples that follow, we shall assume that at least one member of the class represented by our subject ("textbook," "soldier," "coffee," "insect") exists.

A Proposition

An **A** proposition affirms in effect that *every S* comprises *part* of the extension of *P*.

Example: Every textbook is intended for purposes of study.

The intent of this statement is that *"All* textbooks" belong to the class of "things to be studied." However, textbooks do not *exhaust* the class of "things to be studied"—since included in this class are also maps, works of art, and so forth. Hence the predicate is applied to the subject in only *part* of its (the predicate's) extension—that part of it which *includes* the subject. For this reason, then, the predicate is said to be a *particular* or *undistributed* term (see Diagram 5.6).

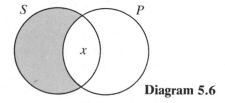

Diagram 5.6

E Proposition

In an **E** proposition the predicate (*P*) is totally excluded from the extension of *S*, and for this reason *P* is taken as a *universal* or distributed term. This is to say that the entire extension of *S* lies outside the *P* circle *taken in its entirety* (Diagram 5.7).

Example: No true soldier is a coward.

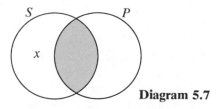

Diagram 5.7

I Proposition

An **I** proposition affirms that an indeterminate portion of the extension of S comprises part of the extension of P.

Example: Some coffee is imported.

Here, as in the **A** proposition, the predicate is affirmed of the subject but, again, in only *part* of its (the predicate's) extension. The predicate, therefore, is *particular,* or *undistributed* (Diagram 5.8).[1]

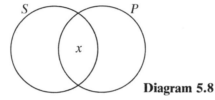

Diagram 5.8

O Proposition

In an **O** proposition the predicate, as taken in its *complete* extension, is *denied* of the subject (*some S*).

Example: Some insects are not poisonous.

The **O** proposition states in effect that the predicate, in its complete extension, is to be excluded from a portion of S, namely, that portion of S which we are considering (Diagram 5.9).[2]

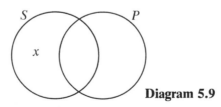

Diagram 5.9

---

[1] In this connection we need only mention a point that will be formally treated, under the square of opposition, in Chapter 7. The truth of an **I** proposition is not necessarily incompatible with the possible truth of its corresponding **A**. In stating the **I** proposition, "Some coffee is imported," we do not necessarily rule out the possibility that the **A** proposition, "All coffee is imported," is true. Nor do we, for that matter, *imply* the truth of the O proposition, "Some coffee is not imported."

[2] Here, too, it should be noted that the truth of an **O** proposition is not *necessarily* incompatible with the possible truth of its corresponding **E;** nor does it imply the truth of the **I** proposition.

Chart 5.1 sums up both the quantity of terms and the quality of propositions as studied thus far in this chapter.

Chart 5.1

Type of Proposition	Quantity of S	Quality of C	Quantity of P
A	Universal	Affirmative	Particular
E	Universal	Negative	Universal
I	Particular	Affirmative	Particular
O	Particular	Negative	Universal

EXERCISE 5.1

A. Answer the following.

1. What is the general rule for determining the quantity of a proposition?
2. (a) What is meant by an *indesignate proposition?* (b) How does one judge the quantity of this type?
3. What is the general rule for determining the quality of a proposition?
4. Give the two rules for determining the quantity of the predicate term.
5. What is the extensional relationship of *S* and *P* in each of the four types of propositions (**A, E, I,** and **O**)?

B. Use a Venn diagram to express each of the following propositions.

1. Some men are not bald.
2. No man is an island.
3. All those who act without thinking are pitiful human beings.
4. Two of the girls died in a plane crash.
5. Some men are impatient for death.
6. All elephants are not obese. (Hint: this is not an **A** proposition.)
7. Some white mice are not tiny.
8. Several emperors were assassinated.
9. Some dwarfs are chubby.
10. All mermaids are sirens.

LOGICAL FORM

Since many propositions are rather loosely construed, it is often necessary to clarify their basic logical structures. In general, to put a proposition into its logical form is to reconstruct it to conform to one of the typical patterns: "Every *S* is *P*"; "No *S* is *P*"; and so on. Or, if no sign of quantity is required—as, for example, in singular propositions—it simply takes the form: "*S* is (or is not) *P*."

Here special attention should be given to the "tricky **O**." Frequently an **O** statement is expressed in some such form as: "Not all," "Not every," or even "All are not." In all such cases, simply restate the proposition in the form *"Some S is not P."*

Example: Not all men are procrastinators.

As a means of determining more exactly the form of a proposition, we should consider each of the following four possibilities:

1.   *S*   c   *P*
2. non-*S*   c   *P*
3.   *S*   c non-*P*
4. non-*S*   c non-*P*

Here it is important to note that any of the propositions we have treated may take any of the forms above. For example, an **A** proposition might read "All non-*S* is non-*P*. The negations within the terms do not of themselves make a proposition negative; whether a proposition is affirmative or negative is determined in each case by the quality of the verb.

EXERCISE 5.2

A. Work out the following:

1. Generally speaking, what is meant by putting a proposition in its *logical* form?
2. What are some of the typical nonlogical expressions of the **O** proposition?
3. Show that it is inadvisable to express an **E** proposition in the form "All *S* is not *P*."
4. Make up a list of ten examples of **A, E, I,** and **O** propositions in which you illustrate the following forms: "*S* is (not) *P*"; "non-*S* is (is not) *P*"; "*S* is (is not) non-*P*"; "non-*S* is (is not) non-*P*."

B. The following are simple categoricals. Examine these statements for their meaning and discuss them. Decide in each case if the proposition is **A, E, I,** or **O,** and for the sake of practice give your own version of the logical form whenever the need exists. If a proposition is singular, regard it as **A** or **E**, depending on whether it affirms or denies. In the case of indesignates, decide for yourself whether the statement is universal or particular.

1. Most Americans have no idea of what it means to go hungry.
2. All the batteries in this flashlight are dead.
3. Some non-students are playboys.
4. Some non-playboys are good students.
5. No good student is a playboy.
6. Creativity is a native endowment.
7. No genius is an uncreative person.
8. All non-creative persons are non-geniuses.
9. No creative person is a numbskull.
10. Violence breeds violence.
11. All nominalists are non-realists.
12. No non-realist is a nominalist.
13. Some of my friends are incurable optimists.
14. Others are hopeless pessimists.
15. All non-day-school students are evening students.
16. No evening school student is a non-adult.
17. Amnesia is an embarrassing malady to have.
18. Not to remember who your friends are is the best way of losing them.
19. Some people are highly introspective.
20. No introspective person is of the unreflecting sort.
21. Most professors drive me crazy. (Do not transcribe: "Most professors are crazy-drivers.")
22. Right field is a lonely position.
23. No non-hypochondriac worries about his health.
24. All hypochondriacs worry about their health.
25. Most people who do not worry about their health stay healthy.
26. Victorianism is a thing of the past.
27. Some fears are groundless.
28. Inexpensive items are not worth preserving.
29. Every class has its clowns.
30. Some clowns lack class.
31. Mountain climbing is a good hobby for youngsters.
32. "What youth longs for is a bore to old age" (Emerson).
33. Not all inexplicable events are miraculous.
34. Broiling steak in the oven is a good deal easier than cooking it outdoors.

35. A marathon is something that lasts as long as you can make it last.

COMPOUND STATEMENTS

As opposed to the single categorical, a compound proposition is a sentence expressing more than one object of assent. Such propositions contain more than one logical subject or predicate or more than one of both.

Example: John F. Kennedy and Lyndon B. Johnson were both Democratic presidents.

Such propositions need not be broken down into their components, especially if their meaning is clear and their truth apparent. In actual practice, however, there are many propositions—"package" statements—that should be broken down for the purpose of examining their meaning, their truth value, or both. Take, for example, the statement: "Though neither Mussolini nor Hitler were Italians, they were both fanatical leaders of the Third Reich." To agree with this statement, you must agree with everything it says, which is to say that the truth of such a statement depends on the truth of all its parts. If any part of such a statement is false, then the statement as a whole is false. Accordingly, whenever you encounter such a statement—let us say, in a true-or-false examination—you should always mark it "false."

EXERCISE 5.3

On the basis of your general knowledge, evaluate the following statements as true or false.

1. Plato and Kant were both Greek philosophers and both of them were idealists.
2. New York, New Jersey, and Hawaii are all part of the continental United States.
3. Lincoln and Charlemagne were both great statesmen of the nineteenth century.
4. Philosophy and literature are both considered liberal arts.
5. Both Theodore and Franklin Roosevelt were presidents of the United States.

With particular respect to compound statements, the reader should know that it is part of the business of critical thinking to distinguish the false from the true, the meretricious from the authentic, the misleading statement from the one that is true to the facts. Unfortunately it is seldom the case that either truth or falsity is presented in its pure, unvarnished form.

chapter 6

Opposition

The Meaning of Opposition
Rules of Opposition
Practical Observations
Compounds

To know the meaning of a proposition is one thing and to know its implication is another. In this chapter we shall see what propositions imply under the "square of opposition."

THE MEANING OF OPPOSITION

The term *opposition* in logic is applied to the relationship of propositions that have the *same subject and predicate terms:*

1. *Every* toll bridge *is* expensive.	(**A** proposition)
2. *No* toll bridge *is* expensive.	(**E** proposition)
3. *Some* toll bridges *are* expensive.	(**I** proposition)
4. *Some* toll bridges *are not* expensive.	(**O** proposition)

In relation to proposition 1, for instance, proposition 2 differs (or is opposed) in *quality* but not in quantity. Proposition 3 is opposed to proposition 1 in *quantity,* although not in quality. Proposition 4 is opposed to proposition 1 in *both quantity and quality.* The following, are the four different kinds of opposition:

> *Contrary opposition* is that between two *universals* of different quality (**A** and **E**).
> *Subcontrary opposition* is that between two *particulars* of *different quality* (**I** and **O**).
> *Subaltern opposition* is that between *a universal and a particular* of the *same quality* (**A** and **I**; **E** and **O**).[1]

---

[1] We are somewhat stretching the meaning of the term "opposition" when we use it to describe the relation that exists between subalterns. Actually, subalterns are

Contradictory opposition is that between *a universal and a particular* of *different quality* (**A** and **O**; **E** and **I**).

To represent the different types of opposition, logicians make use of a traditional diagram, referred to as the *square of opposition* (see Diagram 6.1). As a preliminary exercise, refer to the diagram and determine which of the four types of opposition exists between each of the following sets:

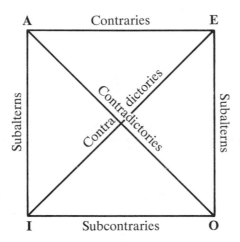

Diagram 6.1

All politicians are honest.
No politicians are honest.

Some housewives are good cooks.
Some housewives are not good cooks.

Some wars are futile.
Some wars are not futile.

No civilization is amoral.
Some civilization is not amoral.

Some harvests are plentiful.
All harvests are plentiful.

Some poetry is not sentimental.
All poetry is sentimental.

---

compatible both in truth and in falsity, even though they differ in their *quantity*. It is only in this latter sense that they are said to be opposed and can therefore be represented on the square of opposition.

RULES OF OPPOSITION

The standard procedure in applying the square of opposition is to begin with a proposition that is *given as true or false,* with a view toward determining whether its corresponding contradictory, contrary, subcontrary, or subaltern is true, false, or doubtful. Thus, if it is *true* that *"All* good men are virtuous," is the *contradictory* proposition, *"Some* good men are not virtuous," *true, false,* or *doubtful?*

Contradictory Opposition (A–O; E–I)

Contradictory Propositions Cannot Both Be True

The rule that contradictories cannot both be true supposes, *as does the first in each of the groups that follow,* that the initial proposition is *given as true.* According to the rule just stated, if any proposition is *given as true,* its corresponding contradictory must be *false.* If, for example, an **I** proposition is true, then its **E** variant must be false.

(**I**)	Some homes are expensive.	(*given as true*)
(**E**)	No home is expensive.	(*false*)

Contradictory Propositions Cannot Both Be False

The rule that contradictories cannot both be false supposes, *as does the second in each of the groups that follow,* that the initial proposition is given as *false.* If any proposition is given as *false,* its corresponding contradictory must be *true.* Thus, if an **A** proposition is false, then its **O** variant is necessarily true.

(**A**)	Every nuisance is a bore.	(*given as false*)
(**O**)	Some nuisances are not bores.	(*true*)

We note that the rules of contradictory opposition are the easiest to apply because there is no room here for doubt. Further, *contradictory opposition* is opposition in the *complete, unqualified sense of the term.*

To sum up: *Contradictories are incompatible both in truth and in falsity.*

Contrary Opposition (A–E)

Contrary Propositions Cannot Both Be True

The initial proposition that is given as true is an **A** or an **E**, and the question is simply: If **A** is true, what can be implied of its **E** variant (that is, its contrary)? Is it true, false, or doubtful? Conversely, if **E** is true, what is to be said of its **A** variant? The rule states quite simply that contraries *cannot* both be true. It follows, then, that if one contrary is *given as true,* then its corresponding contrary must be *false.* Thus, if **A** is true, **E** must be false. For example:

> **(A)**   Every democracy respects human rights.   (*given as true*)
> **(E)**   No democracy respects human rights.   (*false*)

Conversely, if **E** is true, then **A** must be false:

> **(E)**   No child is a criminal.   (*give as true*)
> **(A)**   Every child is a criminal.   (*false*)

Contrary Propositions Can Both Be False

According to the rule, contraries (**A** and **E** propositions) *can* both be false. Does this mean that if one contrary is *given as false* the other *must be* false? Clearly not, for if contraries *can* or *may* both be false, and one is *given as false,* the other is doubtful.[2] Given as false the **E** proposition:

> No man is a coward.

Its **A** variant is:

> Every man is a coward.

But this is *doubtful.* (Even though we may know this proposition to be false as a matter of fact, we cannot *imply* that it is.)

By way of summary: *contraries are incompatible in truth but compatible in falsity.*

---

[2] Keep in mind that *whenever* a rule says "can" or "may," there is no necessary implication, and from a logical point of view this means "doubtful."

Subcontrary Opposition (I-O)

Subcontrary Propositions Can Both Be True

We have seen that contraries cannot both be true. The rule is just the reverse for subcontraries: both *can* be true. By way of application it follows that, *given a subcontrary as true,* there is no implication as to the truth or falsity of its corresponding subcontrary. Since the rule states that subcontraries can be true together, and if, as a matter of fact, one of them *is* true, then the other *may* be true or false. Hence, it is doubtful. Given the truth of the **I** proposition:

> Some candy is hard to chew.

Its **O** variant is *doubtful,* even though it may be true *as a matter of fact* that

> Some candy is not hard to chew.

Again, given as true the **I** proposition:

> Some logic texts deal with inference.

The **O** variant is doubtful on the basis of mere implication, even though in this case it is *false* that

> Some logic texts do not deal with inference.

In view of the common-sense supposition that the truth of an **I** proposition implies the truth of its **O** variant (and conversely), an explanation is in order here to account for the discrepancy between the point of view of logic and that of common sense. Why is it that common sense favors such an implication, whereas logic does not?

The reason for this difference is rooted in the fact that common-sense judgments are purely *practical* as opposed to *scientific.* A purely practical judgment is one that settles a doubt (if doubt there be) on the basis of what is considered more or less *probable* or *likely.* Sometimes, too, an appeal is made to the "law of averages" or even to statistics. Applying this consideration to our present problem, we find that the common-sense implication from the truth of an **I** proposition to the truth of an **O** (and vice versa) amounts to this: If **I** is true, it is *likely* or *probable* that **O** also is true. In actual fact, it *usually* turns out that both propositions are true. Such judgments, however, are far from infallible. Strictly speaking, there is room here for doubt, and this is precisely the point of view of logic. From a scientific point of view there is no theoretical (logical) necessity involved in judging that if "Some *S* is *P*," then "Some *S* is not *P*." Hence, there is no room for any *formal* implication.[3]

Subcontrary Propositions Cannot Both Be False

Whereas contraries may both be false, this condition does not apply to subcontraries. Given the falsity of any subcontrary, its corresponding subcontrary must be *true*. From the falsity of the **O** proposition, "Some men do not have emotions," we must imply the truth of its **I** variant. Or, given the falsity of the **I** proposition, "Some monkeys are human," the **O** variant is necessarily true. To sum up: *Subcontraries are compatible in truth but incompatible in falsity.*

Subaltern Opposition (A–I; E–O)

In the relationship of subalterns the universal proposition is spoken of as the subalter*nant,* the particular, as the subalter*nate.* The two propositions when taken together are called *subalterns.*

> *If the univeral is true, its subalternate (particular)*
> *is likewise true; if its subalternate (particular) is*
> *true, the universal is doubtful.*

It is perfectly legitimate to pass from the truth of the universal to the truth of the particular, but not conversely. Hence, if an **A** proposition is true, its **I** variant is necessarily true. For example:

All cactus plants are thorny.   (*given as true*)
Some cactus plants are thorny.   (*true*)

The truth of the particular is *contained* in the truth of the universal. It would be wrong, however, to imply the truth of the universal from the truth of the **I** proposition. For example:

Some convicts are innocent.   (*given as true*)
Every convict is innocent.   (*doubtful*)

---

[3] On this last point the student must be fully aware that if *any* implication or inference is to be valid, it must *necessarily follow*—that is, according to a strict *logical* necessity—from what is laid down. If no such necessity is involved, there is simply no implication, and if any implication were drawn, it would be invalid.

> *If the universal is false, its subalternate (particular) is doubtful; if its subalternate (particular) is false, the universal is false.*

This rule in effect states that if the universal is false, the particular may be either true or false; one does not know. If, on the other hand, the particular is false, it follows *for all the more reason* that the universal is false. If an **A** proposition is false, its **I** variant is *doubtful*. For example:

All jets are on schedule.	(*given as false*)
Some jets are on schedule.	(*doubtful*)

If, however an **I** proposition is false, then its **A** variant is certainly false. Thus:

Some dogs are centipedes.	(*given as false*)
All dogs are centipedes.	(*false*)

Chart 6.1 is a summary of conclusions derivable from the square of opposition. The student should examine each conclusion of this chart and cite the appropriate rule that governs it. Then he should close the text and reconstruct the chart on the basis of the rules just studied.

Chart 6.1

	A is	E is	I is	O is
If **A** is true		F *	T	F
If **E** is true	F		F	T
If **I** is true	D	F		D
If **O** is true	F	D	D	
If **A** is false		D	D	T
If **E** is false	D		T	D
If **I** is false	F	T		T
If **O** is false	T	F	T	

* *Key:* T, true; F, false; D, doubtful.

PRACTICAL OBSERVATIONS

The chief practical utility of the square of opposition is to enable the user to know how to *refute* a given proposition, for it is during refutation that the most flagrant blunders in a discussion or a debate are committed.

To avoid these blunders, we should note first that *the only propositions that are incompatible in their truth are contraries and contradictories.* The only way to refute any proposition, therefore, is to establish the truth of either its *contrary* or its *contradictory.* If this can be done, obviously the proposition of one's opponent is shown to be false.

In this connection it should be noted that one does *not* refute an **I** or an **O** proposition by setting up its subcontrary. This point would be too obvious to mention were it not for the fact that persons sometimes "argue" (much to their own distress and others' amusement) somewhat in the following fashion: "You claim that some of the athletes on our team are *not* good sports. Well, it's my own contention that most of them *are,* and if you want me to prove it to you, I can." It goes without saying that even if the person making the above statement *proves* his contention, in itself this is not enough to *disprove* the subcontrary statement against which he is arguing, for *subcontraries may both be true.*

A moment ago we said that the only way to refute a proposition is to establish either the contrary or the contradictory. We should now make it clear that, although it is *possible* to disprove a proposition by its contrary, doing so is neither necessary nor, as a rule, advisable. Clearly, if we can show that our proposition (which is the contrary of our opponent's) is true, then we have refuted our opponent's position, since *contraries cannot both be true.* The point of the present consideration, however, is to emphasize the equally important fact that *contraries can both be false.* Thus, there is the ever-present danger of opposing one false proposition *with another* that is also *false.* Let us suppose that someone is attempting to establish the following proposition:

All economic activity should be in the hands of the government.

Not infrequently, in such a case an opponent may think it necessary to prove the contrary:

No economic activity should be in the hands of the government.

If this second proposition could be proved to be true, it would obviously serve to refute in very strong terms the one to which it is opposed. In actual fact, however, the second proposition may well turn out to be as false as the original, since *contraries can both be false.* At least, one should be very certain of his ground before he attempts to refute one contrary by means of another, for most often "he who proves too much, proves nothing."

To attempt to refute one subcontrary proposition by means of another is therefore no refutation at all, because subcontraries can both be true. To attempt to refute one contrary by means of another is to resort to a risky means of refutation, because contraries can both be false.

In line with these considerations, then, it should be noted as a cardinal rule of logic that the only requirement to refute *any* proposition is to establish the truth of its *contradictory*.

Thus, all that is necessary to refute the proposition, *"All* economic activity should be in the hands of the government," is to establish the following (contradictory): *"Some* economic activity should *not* be in the hands of the government."

Under most circumstances the only sane, practical way to refute a proposition is to establish its contradictory. Under all circumstances this is all that is necessary.

EXERCISE 6.1

A. Work out the following.

1. Define each of the four types of opposition.
2. Cite the appropriate rules for each of these four types.
3. According to one of the rules, the truth of the universal subalternant cannot be implied from the truth of the particular subalternate. Do you think this rule is frequently violated in practice? If so, exemplify.
4. (a) Discuss some of the mistakes that are commonly made with regard to the "logic of refutation." (b) In what way or ways should your knowledge of opposition help you to avoid these mistakes?

B. Decide whether the following are correct or incorrect.

1. Given an **O** proposition as false, its **A** variant is doubtful.
2. Given an **O** proposition as true, its **I** variant is false.
3. Given an **E** proposition as false, its **A** variant is doubtful.
4. Given an **I** proposition as true, its **A** variant is doubtful.
5. Given an **E** proposition as true, its **I** variant must be false.

C. On the basis of the square of opposition, determine whether the corresponding variants (**A, E, I,** or **O**) are true, false, or doubtful.

1. Given as *false:* Some universities are not institutions of higher learning.
2. Given as *true:* Some drugs cause damage to the brain.
3. Given as *false:* No theologian is a philosopher.
4. Given as *false:* Some events are uncaused.
5. Given as *true:* All children are young.

D. Work out the following.

    1. Given a *true* **A,** tell what its variants are.
    2. Given a *false* **A,** tell what its variants are.
    3. Given a *true* **E,** tell what its variants are.
    4. Given a *false* **E,** tell what its variants are.

E. What proposition must be established to refute the following statements?

    1. No politician is a prevaricator.
    2. All college students are abnormal.
    3. Some dog is not a mammal.
    4. All cats have tails.
    5. Some history does not refer to the past.

COMPOUNDS [4]

Compound statements are not ordinarily susceptible to a fourfold scheme of opposition as are single categoricals. It is nevertheless good to know how to contradict them as the need arises. The most ordinary practical means of contradicting compound statements is to show that the part with which one disagrees is wrong. Thus, "Mother and Dad are both over forty" may be contradicted by stating, "Mother is not over forty." Another way of denying them is by an "either-or" type of statement. Thus, "Mother and Dad are both over forty" may be denied by saying, "Either Mother is not over forty or Dad is not." To state in this instance that neither of them is over forty might be going too far, since this would be a contrary rather than a contradictory statement. Note that since compound statements of this sort (conjunctives) depend for their truth on the truth of *all* their parts, for purposes of denial it is sufficient to show that only *one* of the parts is false.

Compound statements may also be denied by the use of the expression, "It is not the case that such-and-such is so." And for purposes of symbolic logic it is not too early to begin with the proper means of denial of such propositions. Suppose, for example, I say that

    Men are strong and women are fair.

Symbolically, I might represent this proposition as follows:

$$M \cdot W$$

---

    [4] Reference is made in this chapter, not to every type of compound statement (for example, the "If . . . then" type), but only to those multiple categoricals whose truth depends on the truth of each and all of the parts.

Here the dot (·) is used to signify "and." To deny this proposition as a whole, I would put it in parentheses and prefix it with a negative sign:

$$\sim (M \cdot W)$$

This is equivalent to saying, "It is not the case that men are strong and women are fair." In a later chapter we shall study in greater detail the symbolism used for these and other types of statements.

Some special attention should be given here to the denial of what are known as *exclusive* and *exceptive* statements.

Exclusive Statements

"Only gum chewers will be excluded from the show." Here it would be awkward and confusing to assert by denial, "Not only gum chewers will be excluded." Accordingly, we should first break the statement down into its parts and then deny it. Thus:

> Gum chewers will be excluded.
> No non-gum chewer will be excluded.

To deny the statement, say that either some gum chewers will *not* be excluded or that some gum chewer *will* be excluded.

Exceptive Statements

An exceptive statement says something like "All the money except yours has been found." Deny this statement by denying the exception ("At least some of my money has been found") or by denying the main part of the statement ("Someone else's money has not been found").

> *Further Examples:*
> Only John will be admitted (exclusive).
> > *Sample denials.* John will not be admitted (or) Someone *else* (besides John) will be admitted.
> Money alone will bring you the joys of life.
> > *Sample Denials.* Money will not bring you the joys of life (or) Something else (like friendship) is needed.
> Everyone except Zeke knows how to dance.
> > *Sample denials.* Zeke *does* know how to dance (or) Someone else (besides him) does not.

EXERCISE 6.2

Deny as you think best the following compound statements.

1. Logic and golf are both liberal arts.
2. Neither you nor I knows the answer.
(Suppose someone says, "We *both* know the answer." Is this a simple denial?)
3. Only Communists are radicals.
4. All snakes except rattlesnakes are poisonous.
(What if someone says, "Rattlesnakes are the *only* ones that are poisonous"?)
5. All students except freshmen are intelligent.

It is not necessary or practical for an elementary text in logic to present all the possible variations derivable from the square of opposition. The most important ones have been indicated. The student need only remember that whatever the type of proposition handled, it is always according to the same set of rules.

chapter 7

Obversion and Conversion

Obversion

Conversion

Combined Forms

Emotional Statements: How to Interpret Their Meaning

In our study of opposition we have seen that statements not only mean something but imply other things as well. The purpose of this chapter is to examine further methods of implication that take us beyond the square of opposition: *obversion, conversion, and the combined forms.* By "combined forms" we mean various ways in which we combine obversion and conversion, once they have been learned as separate processes; combined forms are *contraposition* and *inversion.*

The advantage of this section of logic may be seen from the fact that people often attach an interpretation to a statement that is in no way justified by the statement itself. As a means of avoiding such faulty procedure, there is no better method than knowing which implications follow from a given statement and which do not.

In our discussion of contradictory opposition we set up propositions that were opposed to each other in meaning. Not so with obversion, conversion, and their combined forms; our only intent here is to derive from a given proposition a second statement which is consistent in meaning with the original. The second statement will, of course, differ from the first in form—in the way it is expressed—but not essentially in its meaning. Thus, wherever the first statement is true, the second must likewise be true.

OBVERSION

Let us begin, then, with *obversion,* a simple process of taking an affirmative proposition and making it contain the same meaning in negative form; the reverse—turning a negative into its affirmative—is also obversion. The original statement is called the *obvertend;* the derived statement, the *obverse.*

OBVERTEND	(**A**)	All of this food is edible.	(*true*)
OBVERSE	(**E**)	None of this food is inedible.	(*true*)

Rules of Obversion

Rule 1: **Leave the subject as is.**
Rule 2: **Contradict the copula.**
Rule 3: **Contradict the predicate.**

$$
\begin{array}{ccc}
S & is & P. \\
S & is\ not & \text{non-}P. \\
(Rule\ 1) & (Rule\ 2) & (Rule\ 3)
\end{array}
$$

The application of Rule 1 is obvious, though Rules 2 and 3 will need a little explanation.

> *If one of the conventional prefixes or suffixes is misleading, attach the prefix "non" to the original word as a means of contradicting it.*

Kinds of Obversion

An **A** *Proposition Obverts to an* **E**

OBVERTEND	(**A**)	All skilifts are comfortable.
OBVERSE	(**E**)	No skilifts are uncomfortable.

An **E** *Proposition Obverts to an* **A**

Do the reverse of the above.

An **I** *Proposition Obverts to an* **O**

OBVERTEND	(**I**)	Some sayings are nonsensical.
OBVERSE	(**O**)	Some sayings are not the kind that make sense.

An **O** *Proposition Obverts to an* **I**

Do the reverse of the above.

Sample Forms

OBVERTEND	(**A**)	All	non-*S*	is		non-*P*.
OBVERSE	(**E**)	No	non-*S*	is		*P*.
OBVERTEND	(**E**)	No	*S*	is		*P*.
OBVERSE	(**A**)	All	*S*	is		non-*P*.
OBVERTEND	(**I**)	Some	non-*S*	is		non-*P*.
OBVERSE	(**O**)	Some	non-*S*	is not		*P*.
OBVERTEND	(**O**)	Some	non-*S*	is not	non-*P*.
OBVERSE	(**I**)	Some	non-*S*	is		*P*.

The chief practical advantage of obversion lies in its clarification of the positive implications of purely negative statements. Thus, the statement "War is not without its ethical implications," asserts that war does have ethical implications.

EXERCISE 7.1

Obvert the following.

1. All balloons are inflatable.
2. All impoverished people are without money.
3. Some hangers-on at the university are non-students.
4. Today is my unbirthday.
5. Some murder mysteries are not unsolvable.

CONVERSION

Conversion is essentially a process of *interchanging the subject and predicate terms* of a given proposition in such a way that the derived proposition (the converse) is consistent with the meaning of the original (the convertend). Offhand, this may appear to be a rather arbitrary procedure—as, indeed, it would be, were we to proceed without a set of rules. For example, it does not make much sense to say that "Because rabbits eat carrots, therefore carrots eat rabbits" or "Because Ron is riding his horse, therefore his horse is riding Ron." Our first step, therefore, is to set up our proposition in logical form; then we convert it:

CONVERTEND	(Some) rabbits eat carrots.
	(Logical form: Some rabbits are carrot-eaters.)
CONVERSE	Some carrot-eaters are rabbits.

EXERCISE 7.2

Before studying the rules, try converting the following. (Do not be surprised if you come up with some strange results.)

1. Bill rides a motorcycle to school.
2. No one who hates athletics is a sport.
3. Some cars are not Chevrolets.
4. Some smokers like cigars.
5. All children are human beings.

Rules of Conversion

Any attempt to convert the above propositions points to the need for the two following rules:

Rule 1: Keep the quality of the converse the same as that of the convertend.
Rule 2: In converting a proposition, never overextend a term.

Rule 1 is the easiest to apply: if a statement is affirmative, *keep* it affirmative in the converse; if the original is negative, keep it negative in the converse. For example, **A** or **I** would never convert to an **E** or **O,** but they can convert to another affirmative proposition.

Rule 2 ("never overextend a term") will take some further explanation. To understand what the rule means, refresh your mind with the following chart of results from our study of Chapter Five. Recall that each term of a categorical statement is either universal or particular, as follows:

(**A**)   All S^u is P^p.
(**E**)   No S^u is P^u.
(**I**)   Some S^p is P^p.
(**O**)   Some S^p is not P^u.

If a term is particular in the convertend and it is *made universal* in the converse, it has been "overextended."

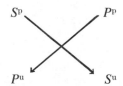

overextended   overextended

Note: Sometimes the quantity of a term may be reduced in the process of conversion—that it, it is converted from a universal to a particular. The Rule forbids only an *over*extension of terms.

Kinds of Conversion

Conversion of an **A** *Proposition*

The importance of conversion lies in the method of converting an **A** proposition, for it is here that Rule 2 is most frequently violated. Thus it is sometimes thought that because all scientific knowledge is organized, *therefore,* all organized knowledge is scientific. Such a conclusion may, of course, seem logical, as do most fallacies of implication, but let us put it to the test:

$$S^u \qquad\qquad\qquad P^p$$
CONVERTEND **(A)**   *All*   scientific   knowledge   is   organized.
$$\qquad\quad P^p \qquad\qquad\qquad S^p$$
CONVERSE   **(I)**   *Some* organized knowledge   is   scientific.

Since the predicate term of our convertend (an **A** proposition) is particular, in transposing it—that is, in making it the subject of the converse—we must *keep it particular.* Since the subject of the converse, then, is a particular term, the converse itself is a particular **(I)** proposition. Thus *"All S is P"* becomes *"Some P is S."*

Conversion of an **E** *Proposition*

In converting an **E** proposition, it is impossible to overextend a term, since both **S** and **P** are universal to begin with.

CONVERTEND **(E)**   No scientist is an ignorant person.
CONVERSE   **(E)**   No ignorant person is a scientist.

Care must be taken, however, in the conversion of propositions that involve a negation within one or both of the terms. Consider the following proposition:

A person who is not virtuous is not happy.

This proposition does *not* convert to

No happy person is virtuous.

But it *does* convert to

> No happy person is nonvirtuous.

Conversion of an I Proposition

An **I** proposition converts to another **I.**

> CONVERTEND **(I)**   Some ignorant people are prejudiced.
> CONVERSE   **(I)**   Some prejudiced people are ignorant.

O *Propositions Do Not Convert*

It may seem perfectly legitimate to imply that because "Some detectives are not policemen," therefore "Some policemen are not detectives." Granted the independent truth of these statements, the second is not the *converse* of the first. The attempted conversion of the above example is as invalid as the following:

> Some Americans are not New Yorkers.
> Some New Yorkers are not Americans.
>
> Some engines are not gas-propelled.
> Some gas-propelled objects are not engines.

Rule 2 of conversion forbids the conversion of an **O** proposition. Suppose an **O** proposition as convertend and another **O** as the converse; note below the overextension of the subject term of the original proposition when it appears as predicate of the converse:

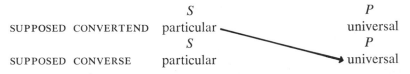

	S	*P*
SUPPOSED CONVERTEND	particular	universal
SUPPOSED CONVERSE	*S* particular	*P* universal

As in the example above, it is as important for the student to know when no implication can be made as it is for him to make a correct implication when it is justified.

Sample Forms

> CONVERTEND   **(A)**   All   non-*S*   is   *P.*
> CONVERSE   **(I)**   Some   *P*   is   non-*S.*

CONVERTEND	(**E**)	No	non-*S*	is	non-*P*.
CONVERSE	(**E**)	No	non-*P*	is	non-*S*.
CONVERTEND	(**I**)	Some	*S*	is	non-*P*.
CONVERSE	(**I**)	Some	non-*P*	is	*S*.

In the examples above, note that the original *forms of the terms are retained as given; only their position is changed.*

EXERCISE 7.3

Convert the following if they can be converted. (To do a correct job of conversion, do not merely place the verb in the passive voice.)
1. All motorcycles are noisy.
2. Most teenagers enjoy popular music.
3. No accident merely "happens."
4. Some logic students are not "phys-ed" majors.
5. All psychology majors are not interested in philosophy.
6. Some honor students find it hard to keep up their grades.
7. Some men who love computers do not love their wives.
8. All publicity-conscious people are egomaniacs.
9. Most non-extroverts think only about themselves.
10. Cats eat mice.

COMBINED FORMS

It is possible to combine obversion and conversion in various ways; these look more difficult than they are. We shall here concentrate on three of these processes: partial contraposition (PC); full contraposition (FC); (full) inversion (INV).

Partial Contraposition

The partial contrapositive of a proposition is obtained by obverting *and* converting (oc) *as a continuous process* thus:

ORIGINAL	(**A**)	All	*S*	is	*P*	
OBVERT TO	(**E**)	No	*S*	is	non-*P*	
CONVERT TO	(**E**)	No	non-*P*	is	*S*	(PC)

Note: The partial contrapositive (PC) of an **A** is **E**; of an **E** is **I**; of an **O** is **I**. An **I** does not admit of a partial contrapositive. By direct process "All *S* is *P*" becomes "No non-*P* is *S*"; or, as a further example, "All non-*S* is non-*P*" becomes "No *P* is non-*S*."

EXERCISE 7.4

A. Work out the partial contrapositive of the following.

   1. ORIGINAL (**A**)   All revolutionaries are radicals.
   2. ORIGINAL (**E**)   No Roman is a Parisian.
   3. ORIGINAL (**O**)   Some cat is not a Siamese.

B. The following are correct forms of partial contraposition. Go over these examples on paper to understand how they were derived.

   1. ORIGINAL (**A**)   All practical men are realists.
      PARTIAL CONTRAPOSITIVE (**E**) No non-realist is a practical man.
   2. ORIGINAL (**E**)   No moron is a creative person.
      PARTIAL CONTRAPOSITIVE (**I**) Some non-creative person is a moron.
   3. ORIGINAL (**O**)   Some students are not playboys.
      PARTIAL CONTRAPOSITIVE (**I**) Some non-playboys are students.

Note: The validity of all such implications as the above is dependent on the assumption that at least one member each of the S and P classes exists. The same principle holds for any case of obversion, conversion, and the other combined forms we are about to study.

Full Contraposition

If the full contrapositive is worked out on a step-by-step basis, it is obtained by the formula "oco" (obvert, convert, obvert).

Example.

ORIGINAL	(**A**)	All	S	is	P
OBVERT TO	(**E**)	No	S	is	non-P
CONVERT TO	(**E**)	No	non-P	is	S (PC)
OBVERT TO	(**A**)	All	non-P	is	non-S (FC)

Note: The full contrapositive of an **A** is an **A**; of an **E**, an **O**; of an **O**, an **O**. **I** has no full contrapositive. *By direct process* the FC may be derived by reversing the terms of the original statement and by contradicting both of the original terms. Thus "All S is P" becomes "All non-P is non-S." Note, however, that an **E** proposition reduces to an **O**.

Examples.

1. **(A)** All imaginative persons are resourceful.

    (A) All *un*resourceful persons are *un*imaginative. (FC)

2. **(E)** No finite being is perfect.

    (O) Some *im*perfect being is not *in*finite. (FC)

3. **(O)** Some *in*voluntary act is not deliberate.

    (O) Something *in*deliberate is not a voluntary act. (FC)

EXERCISE 7.5

A. Note well that the *full* contrapositive is the partial contrapositive carried one step further. Thus the PC is derived by the formula "oc" (obvert, then convert); the FC by "oco." Accordingly, go back to the examples in Exercise 7.4 and give the full contrapositive.

B. By *direct* process (which is very easy) give the full contrapositive of each of the following:

1. ORIGINAL **(A)**   All neurotics are worriers.
2. ORIGINAL **(E)**   No nominalist is a realist.
3. ORIGINAL **(O)**   Some non-students are not logicians.

Inversion

The (full) inverse of an **A** is worked out by a double process of obversion and conversion (ococ). The inverse of an **E** is worked out by a double process of conversion and obversion (coco). **I** and **O** propositions do not admit of inversion.

ORIGINAL	**(A)**	All	S	is	P	
OBVERT TO	**(E)**	No	S	is	non-P	
CONVERT TO	**(E)**	No	non-P	is	S	(PC)
OBVERT TO	**(A)**	All	non-P	is	non-S	(FC)
CONVERT TO	**(I)**	Some	non-S	is	non-P	(INV)
ORIGINAL	**(E)**	No	S	is	P	
CONVERT TO	**(E)**	No	P	is	S	
OBVERT TO	**(A)**	All	P	is	non-S	
CONVERT TO	**(I)**	Some	non-S	is	P	
OBVERT TO	**(O)**	Some	non-S	is not	non-P	

Note: The inverse of an **A** is **I**; of an **E**, an **O** proposition. If we keep in mind the need for a reduction of quantity (that is, **A** to **I** and **E** to

O), we may work out the inverse of either of these propositions *by direct process,* thus: *contradict* both of the original terms, and leave them in their original position.

Examples:
1. (**A**) All *in*attentive students are *un*deserving of good marks.
   (**I**)   Some attentive students are deserving of good marks. (INV)

2. (**E**) No mature person is *un*stable.
   (**O**) Some *im*mature person is not stable. (INV)

3. (**A**) You claim that All Communists are radicals.
   (**I**)   I imply from this that some *non*-Communists are *non*radicals. (INV).

EXERCISE 7.6

Using the forms as models, invert the statements by direct process.
1. ORIGINAL (**A**)   ALL *S* is *P*.
   INVERSE   (**I**)   SOME non-*S* is non-*P*.

   ORIGINAL (**A**)   All conservatives are traditionalists.
   INVERSE   (**I**)

2. ORIGINAL (**E**)   No *S* is *P*.
   INVERSE   (**O**) Some non-*S* is not non-*P*.

   ORIGINAL (**E**)   No hamster is an elephant.
   INVERSE   (**O**)

EMOTIONAL STATEMENTS: How to Interpret Their Meaning

Much of what we have seen is a kind of mental gymnastics, a self-discipline of the mind, that helps us to grasp the formal elements of logical thought. Logic is more than gymnastics, however, and we must therefore be on our guard for the hidden meanings of statements according to the context in which they are made.

Let us take a sample situation. On July 25, 1967, President de Gaulle of France made a speech in Quebec in which he expressed to a mass audience the hope that Quebec would be *free*. Out of context this statement might have been taken as purely a sign of good will, acceptable to all Canadians. In point of fact, however, the statement was made before an emotionally charged audience that interpreted it to mean that Quebec should be *liberated from* Canada; it was widely believed that the statement was *intended* to carry this meaning. Predictably enough, on the following day Lester Pearson, then Prime Minister of Canada, let it be known that no

Canadian province was in need of liberation, that all were free to begin with, and that de Gaulle's remarks were in any event unacceptable to the Canadian people as a whole. As a result of the incident, the President of France, both to his embarrassment and to that of many others, made an early departure for his native shores.

Situations such as these point to one important fact concerning logic—namely, that propositions often have hidden meanings and must in any case be understood relative to circumstances of time, place, audience, and the total emotional impact of the situation in which they are made. It is with this truth in mind that the reader is invited to determine in what context any given statement is intended to carry what meaning. In any event, the emotional overtones of a statement are often part and parcel of its original intent, and critical thinking requires that we take them into account.

chapter 8

Reasoning

The Purpose of Reasoning
Kinds of Reasoning
Statements of Fact and Necessity
Validity and Truth
The Categorical Syllogism: Its Structure
Axioms

A balanced understanding of logic requires us to see the connection between thought and reality. Logic—elementary logic, at any rate—should never be separated therefore from its moorings in the real world, since it is here that the need for it arises and it is to this area that it is intended to respond. Accordingly, the present chapter is intended to give some insight into the nature of reasoning and into the connection that exists between validity and truth. In the last section of the chapter we will study the basic structure of the categorical structure as well as the axioms that govern its use.

THE PURPOSE OF REASONING

All deductive reasoning takes place—sometimes laboriously—on a step-by-step basis from premises to conclusion. As an act of the mind, reasoning is in no way reducible either to abstraction or to judgment, though it does presuppose both of these prior acts. Without concepts it would be impossible to judge, and without judgments—taken as premises—it would be impossible to reason to a conclusion.

None of the many possible explanations for the necessity of reasoning is more relevant than the fact that man has a natural desire both to know and to increase his existing knowledge. Further, most of us consider it important to use reasoning as a method of leading others to convictions we already hold. Seldom am I satisfied to know *for myself* that Senator Jones would be a good political candidate; I therefore use various means to bring my friends to the same point of view. If I do so by way of argument, then I am reasoning with them. If I employ other methods, I am doing nothing more than expressing my prejudices or opinions.[1]

KINDS OF REASONING

Logicians are generally agreed that there are two basic methods of reasoning; they are respectively known as deduction and induction. Little need be said at this point about the nature of these methods except to suggest that the basis of deductive arguments is generally some statement of principle (however broadly or narrowly conceived) and the basis of inductive arguments is some fact or grouping of facts that are knowable by observation, whether through everyday methods or the methods of scientific inquiry. Further, the conclusion of a deductive argument is generally one that follows by way of necessity from its premises, whereas an inductive conclusion is one that can be established only on probable grounds. As we shall see in Chapter 13, an inductive argument does not begin with premises in the sense that one applies something already known. Rather, you begin with certain key observations and then proceed to construct hypotheses or likely accounts as a method of explaining or verifying the original data. Since our present interest is with deductive reasoning—particularly as it relates to the categorical syllogism—Chapter 13 will give a fuller explanation of induction; what is important at this stage however, is an understanding of the *kind* of statement that lies at the basis of much of our deductive reasoning. Generally speaking, induction—insofar as it depends upon a method of observation—is immediately dependent on what we shall call mere statements of fact. Deduction, however—and categorical reasoning in particular—is more directly dependent on statements of necessity.

STATEMENTS OF FACT AND NECESSITY

The continuing importance for purposes of reasoning between mere statements of fact and those which express necessity should give us further pause. By a "mere statement of fact" we mean one which expresses something that is only *contingently* true or false. For example, I may be right

---

[1] Let it be said that one of the great needs of society today is a return to reason, and with it a return to the conviction that it is by the use of reason that men distinguish themselves as men. This is to say that logic, viewed as a human instrument and not merely as something that can be fed into a computer, can—if conceived in a realistic frame of reference—help pave the way toward what we can hopefully call a "reasonable society."

or wrong in making the statement, "Mary is shopping this afternoon," but whether right or wrong, I mean to express no more than an *empirical truth* —a truth of the sort in which the predicate has no essential connection with the subject to which it is assigned.

Examples of Empirical Statements:
1. John went bowling last night.
2. Tomorrow the President will make a speech.
3. This coffee mug is green.
4. Your trousers need pressing.
5. The television antenna is anchored to the roof.

In each of the above statements nothing in the nature of the subject tells me whether the predicate belongs to it or not. By contrast, however, note the following:

Examples of Necessary Statements:
1. Two and two equal four.
2. The President has the authority to execute the nation's laws.
3. A teacher as such is obliged to help his students to learn.
4. All men have basically equal rights.

Some philosophers would refer to the above statements as "analytical"; this terminology is misleading if it is meant to suggest that they are in no way based on experience. As a matter of fact, every statement has *some* kind of empirical basis. However, our main point is that none of the above statements are *purely* contingent and empirical. Our knowledge of them, though *based* on experience, is based also on our ability to see a connection—that is, some kind of necessary connection—between the subject and predicate terms.

EXERCISE 8.1

Tell whether the following statements are necessarily true, necessarily false, or purely empirical (NT, NF, or PE).

1. Two and two equal nine.
2. Truth and falsity are incompatible.
3. This beggar is poorly clad.
4. A cup is for drinking.
5. My car delivers no more than thirteen miles per gallon.
6. Prices on our new brand of deodorant will be increased tomorrow.

7. A clock is for telling time.

8. None of the Pilgrim Fathers was an Arab.

9. All men are essentially irrational.

10. The television news and weather forecast will be broadcast at ten P.M.

VALIDITY AND TRUTH

In logic we talk a great deal about the "validity" of a reasoning process. In general, a reasoning process is valid only if the conclusion follows from what is laid down in the premises. It is the sole concern of the next few chapters to determine when reasoning is valid and when it is not. As an example, however, of invalid reasoning, note the following:

> All genuine works of art require concentration.
> Everything I study requires concentration.
> Everything I study is a work of art.

Each of these statements may well be true independently of each other, but the last does not follow the first two because the argument as a whole is invalid.

The most important thing, then, for any argument is that it be valid; but its premises should also be true. In the absence of either of these conditions (validity *and* truth of the premises) there is no *guarantee* that the conclusion will be true.

What we have just said is meant to apply to deductive arguments. In the case of induction, where we argue only to a conclusion that is *probably* true, it is possible that even with true premises and a valid argument the conclusion *may* turn out to be false; but we shall take up that matter in a later chapter. Accordingly, chart 8.1 (p. 96) is meant to apply only to deductive arguments.

EXERCISE 8.2

Tell whether you think the following statements are correct or incorrect.

1. If the premises of an argument are true, then the argument as a whole is valid.

2. If an argument is valid, then it must be that the premises are likewise true.

3. If the premises of an argument are true, whether the argument is valid or not, the conclusion is likewise true.

Chart 8.1

	Premises	Conclusion
1	both true	doubtful (true or false)
	reasoning invalid	invalid
2	one or both false	doubtful (true or false)
	reasoning valid	valid (but insignificant)
3	*both true*	*necessarily true*
	reasoning valid	*valid*

4. If the premises of an argument are both true and valid, then the conclusion must likewise be both true and valid.

5. The validity of an argument alone does not assure the truth of the conclusion.

THE CATEGORICAL SYLLOGISM: ITS STRUCTURE

A categorical syllogism consists of three—and only three—propositions and of three—and only three—terms. Take an example:

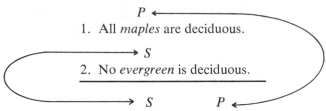

1. All *maples* are deciduous.

2. No *evergreen* is deciduous.

3. No *evergreen* is a *maple*.

Propositions 1 and 2 of the syllogism are its major and minor premises; proposition 3 is the conclusion. As for the *terms* of the syllogism, note carefully that there are three—and only three—terms, even though (and this is an important consideration) *each of them appears twice.*

The above example seeks simply to prove that *No evergreen is a maple* (conclusion). Mark it off therefore as follows:

$$S \qquad P$$

CONCLUSION: No *evergreen* is a *maple*.

The two terms of the conclusion are to be regarded, not only as the *subject* and the *predicate* of the conclusion, but also as the subject and predicate terms of the *syllogism taken as such.* This means that wherever these same terms appear in the premises, they should be regarded as *S* and *P:*

		P		
MAJOR (1):	Every	*maple*	is	deciduous.
		S		
MINOR (2):	No	*evergreen*	is	deciduous.
CONCLUSION (3):	No	*evergreen*	is	a *maple*

In this illustration we place a *P* above "maple" in proposition 1 for the sole reason that it is the very same term which reappears as predicate of the conclusion. The same principle holds for "evergreen" in proposition 2: we mark it *S* because it is the same term that appears as subject of the conclusion.

> *Note:* In this connection observe two important points.
> 1. The *major* premise is so designated because it contains the *P* term of the conclusion.
> 2. The *minor* term is so designated because it contains the *S* term of the conclusion.

So far we have examined two of the three terms of the syllogism—*S* and *P,* each of which appears once in a premise and once in the conclusion. What shall we call the remaining term? Note our example:

	P		*M*
Every	maple	is	*deciduous.*

	S		*M*
No	evergreen	is	*deciduous.*

	S		*P*
No	evergreen	is	a maple.

The remaining term of this syllogism is "deciduous"; we mark it *M* to signify that it functions as the *middle term* (*M* term). By "middle term" we mean one that serves as a point of comparison, as a common standard of reference between *S* and *P*.

Note: The *M* term always appears once in each premise and *never* in the conclusion. Further, the middle term always provides us with the *reason* for what we assert in the conclusion.

EXERCISE 8.3

Give a skeleton of each of the following syllogisms.

Sample: Every collie is a dog.   *Answer:*

M	P
S	M
S	P

No snake is a collie.

No snake is a dog.

As you construct a box like the one above, observe that the conclusion (last part) will always be *S–P*.

1. Every boy is a male.
   Every child in our family is a boy.
   Every child in our family is a male.
2. All paper is combustible.
   No brick is combustible.
   No brick is paper.
3. Every peacock has feathers.
   Every peacock is a bird.
   Some bird has feathers.
4. Every tree is a living thing.
   All living things are organisms.
   Some organism is a tree.

If you have correctly worked out the above examples, you will have noted that the *S, P,* and *M* terms can vary their positions in the premises of the syllogism so as to produce different combinations or patterns, such as *P–M, S–M, S–P;* or *M–P, M–S, S–P*. These different combinations or patterns are known as the *figures* of the syllogism—of which there are only four possible kinds.

	Figure 1	Figure 2	Figure 3	Figure 4
MAJOR:	M–P	P–M	M–P	P–M
MINOR:	S–M	S–M	M–S	M–S
CONCLUSION:	S–P	S–P	S–P	S–P

We also speak of the "mood" of a syllogism, and by this we mean simply the kind of proposition (**A, E, I, O**) that appears as major and minor premise and as conclusion. For example, **AEE** would signify that the major premise is an **A** proposition and that the minor proposition and conclusion are both **E** propositions.

EXERCISE 8.4

Turn back to the previous exercise and specify the mood and figure of each of the four examples you have worked out.

> *Further example:* All philosophers are learned.
> No ignoramus is learned.
> No ignoramus is a philosopher.

The mood of this example is **AEE** and it is cast in Figure 2. In box form it may be represented thus:

A	*P*	*M*
E	*S*	*M*
E	*S*	*P*

AXIOMS

Since Figure 1 (*M–P, S–M*) is the basic figure of the syllogism, it is good to know the axiom that governs its use.

Axiom One

> *Whatever can be affirmed of a logical whole can*
> *be affirmed of its logical parts.*

Let us take "man" as a "logical whole" and say affirmatively, "Man endowed with emotions." In a second step we can say, "Mary is man" (in the sense of being a member of the species). Our third step is simply to re-affirm of the logical part ("Mary") what we already affirmed of the whole ("man")—"Mary is endowed with emotions." The above process is the simplest way of constructing a categorical syllogism in which we set forth a major and a minor premise and a conclusion.

LIBRARY
EMMANUEL SCHOOL OF RELIGION
ONE WALKER DRIVE
JOHNSON CITY, TN 37601

EXERCISE 8.5

Take the following "logical wholes" and construct syllogisms from them according to the model.

1. whale
2. water
3. worm

Axiom Two

> Whatever can be denied of a logical whole can be denied of its logical parts.

Take a logical whole, such as the species horse, and make a universal denial of it: "No horse is a man." Next relate the part to the whole: "Every Percheron is a horse." Finally, deny of the part what you have already denied of the whole: "No Percheron is a man." By a very simple process we have just constructed a syllogism that has a negative conclusion.

EXERCISE 8.6

Use the following "logical wholes" to construct syllogisms according to the negative model.

1. human person
2. cat
3. reptile

Having stated the axioms, we must now proceed to interpret their meaning in greater depth. In the first place it is wrong to think that a syllogism can be constructed from *any* kind of logical whole, as in the following example:

> The United States is a wealthy nation.
> I am a citizen of the United States.
> I am wealthy.

Common sense tells us there is something wrong with this "syllogism," and it is important from a logical standpoint to know why. "The United States" is taken, not as a definite class, but only as a *collective* whole. True

J. SUMMOCK. OR RELIGION
CLUB WALKER DRIVE
JOHNSON CITY, TN. 37601

enough, I *am* a citizen of the United States—but not as though that were part of my nature, as is the case with reference to such concepts as "man." Where, then, does the difference lie? Collective units taken as such are not genuinely logical wholes, whereas such classes as "man," "animal," and "plant" really are. Consider, then, that "man" is universal in the sense that the concept applies to every member of the class. Accordingly, whatever is predicable of man as such (as a *genuine* logical whole) is predicable of each and every man.

One further consideration is in order: no genuine syllogism can result from a mere "counting up" of individuals in the major premise as in the following example:

> All the houses in this block are split-level buildings.
> My house is in this block.
> My house is a split-level building.

The problem in this example is that the "all" of the major premise does not signify a genuine universal but is the result of a mere counting up of each individual house—*including my own.* To reason, then, that *my* house is "split-level" is to do so in a circle because the major premise *presupposes* the very thing it is intending to prove. For any syllogism, then, to be genuine, it must be based on more than a mere counting (a complete enumeration) of particulars; it requires an abstractive insight, however imperfect, into the nature of a thing as such.

EXERCISE 8.7

A. In the light of the above explanation, decide which of the following examples are genuine syllogisms and which are not; show why.

1. T.W.A. spreads out all over the world.
   I am an employee of T.W.A.
   I spread out all over the world.
2. All rattlesnakes are poisonous.
   Some of the snakes in northern Mexico are rattlesnakes.
   Some of the snakes in northern Mexico are poisonous.
3. Every jar in this cabinet is marked with an X.
   This cookie jar is in this cabinet.
   This cookie jar is marked with an X.
4. Our class is intelligent.
   I am a member of our class.
   I am intelligent.

5. All dogs have a sense of smell.
   The German shepherd is a dog.
   The German shepherd has a sense of smell.

B. Make up your own genuine and faulty syllogisms.

chapter 9

The Categorical Syllogism
Rules, Moods, Figures

Statement and Explanation of Rules
Corollaries
Valid Moods
Determining Validity
Using Venn Diagrams

The requirements of syllogistic reasoning, although comparatively few and simple, are extremely important. If logic is to have any significant effect on a student's thinking, observance of the rules must become second nature to him. Nor is it enough simply to learn these rules by rote; the important thing is to put them to proper use.

STATEMENT AND EXPLANATION OF RULES

Most logicians present seven or more rules of the syllogism. It seems a simpler procedure to give the following six and to treat as corollaries two of the statements usually listed as rules. The six rules are:

1. The syllogism should consist of no more than three terms.
2. The middle term must be universal in at least one premise.
3. No term which is particular in a premise may be made universal in the conclusion.
4. No conclusion can be drawn from two negative premises.
5. Two affirmative premises require an affirmative conclusion.
6. A negative premise requires a negative conclusion.

Rule 1: **The syllogism should consist of no more than three terms.**

The importance of the first rule—a requirement of the very structure of the syllogism—derives from the fact that we frequently encounter an arrangement in which there are *apparently* only three, but *actually* four, terms:

> *Example:*
> MAJOR: *A division in the government of a nation* is unfavorable to that nation's welfare.
> MINOR: The legislative, judicial, and executive branches of the United States government are *a division in the government of a nation*.
> CONCLUSION: The legislative, judicial, and executive branches of the United States are (a division) unfavorable to that nation's welfare.

Although our example looks like a three-term construction, it actually contains four terms because of the equivocation in the word "division." The "argument" as it stands is therefore invalid [1] and is reducible to the fallacy of equivocation which we have already discussed under fallacies of language in Chapter 2.

This violation of Rule 1 is contained in the *fallacy of four terms*. Its most typical instance is that in which the *middle term* has diverse and inconsistent meanings, as in the above example. This violation, a particular instance of the fallacy of four terms, is specifically referred to as the *fallacy of the ambiguous middle*. In general, for a syllogism to be valid, the use of the middle term in one premise must be consistent with the use that it has in the other. Here too we should note that the same principle holds for the other terms, *S* and *P;* they should have a basic uniformity of meaning within the particular syllogism.

The more abstract the terms of an argument, the more difficult it becomes to detect the presence of this fallacy. Accordingly, one should, whenever necessary, define the meaning of his terms, especially the kind of terms that appear in the following list:

progress   education
democracy   peace
religion   free enterprise

As a further instance of the ambiguous middle, note the following example:

---

[1] Validity has reference essentially to the *internal consistency of our reasoning acts.* In the case of equivocation, the consistency is destroyed by the fact that a double standard of comparison is used, as in the example above. "Division" in the first sense (as unfavorable to a government's welfare) means an actual split, as during the time of the Civil War; in the second sense (with reference to the parts of a government) it simply means a division of labor and of functions.

The citizens of our community contributed a million dollars to the local charity drive.
John Smith did not contribute a million dollars to the local charity drive.
John Smith is not a citizen of our community.

The function of the middle term in this example is destroyed because in the major premise it is collectively applied to its subject, whereas in the minor it is divisively applied.[2]

EXERCISE 9.1

Each of the following arguments contains some ambiguity. Analyze the source of the problem.

1. No two persons who are arguing from different premises will ever agree on a point of argument. These ladies who live next door to each other are arguing from different premises. Therefore they they will never agree.
2. Logicians keep saying that *all* men are rational. Now the truth of the matter is that most men are not rational. But I hate to admit that most men are not men!
3. All heavy drinkers are inclined to be alcoholic. Most English tea drinkers are heavy drinkers. They are therefore inclined to be alcoholic.
4. All philosophers know something about the history of philosophy, and it is often said that all reasonable men are philosophers. So all reasonable men know something about the history of philosophy.
5. No Democrat is disloyal to his party. But anyone who believes in freedom is a democrat. So no one who believes in freedom is disloyal to his party.

Rule 2: **The middle term must be universal in at least one premise.**

We already know that it is the function of the middle term to serve as a *common point of reference* for uniting or disuniting S and P in the conclusion. Yet if the middle term is taken *particularly* (that is, as an undistributed term) in both premises, there is no guarantee that S and P are being referred to the *same part* of M. Though the rationale of this rule is clear, the practical problem arises of telling *how* the rule is applied. At this point the author will present a method for determining in all instances

---

[2] See Chapter 2 for a discussion of the fallacies of composition and division.

(except for Rule 1 above) whether a categorical syllogism is valid or not.[3] The method we prescribe is this:

1. Determine both the mood and the figure of the syllogism.

Example:
    All men are in need of fresh air.
    All apes are in need of fresh air.
    All apes are men.

The mood of this syllogism is a "triple **A**" (**AAA**), and its figure is No. 2.

MAJOR:	**A**	*P*	*M*
MINOR:	**A**	*S*	*M*
CONCLUSION:	**A**	*S*	*P*

2. The next step is the very important one of marking off the quantity of the terms. To do this, we need to recall what we have already explained in Chapter 5 concerning the quantity of terms in **A, E, I, O** propositions. This can be summed up as follows:

	S	*P*
A	u	p
E	u	u
I	p	p
O	p	u

With the results of the above chart in mind, we can immediately complete our box to represent the example above:

MAJOR:	**A**	P^u	M^p
MINOR:	**A**	S^u	M^p
CONCLUSION:	**A**	S^u	P^p

---

[3] In a subsequent section of this chapter we shall also present the method of determining validity according to Venn diagrams. The advantage of the present method, however, is that it helps us to know *which* fallacy, if any, is involved.

3. Compare the quantity of terms to see if there is a violation of a rule. In the instance above, our syllogism is invalid because the middle term shows up as *"M^pM^p,"* which is to say that it is particular in both of the premises.

EXERCISE 9.2

According to the method prescribed, determine whether the following syllogisms have an undistributed middle.

> 1. No motor vehicle is an apple cart, and some apple carts are primitive. Some primitive objects are not motor vehicles.
> 2. All paper is destructible, and some destructible objects are not edible. Some paper is not edible.
> 3. All beautiful objects are attractive. Some grocery items are attractive. Some grocery items are beautiful.

> *Note:* The middle term must be universal in at least one of the premises, but it needed not be universal in both. The middle must be distributed at least once to establish an adequate point of comparison between *S* and *P*. If the *M* term is particular in both premises, no such comparison is assured.

Rule 3: **No term that is particular in a premise may be made universal in the conclusion.**

Rule 3 is the counterpart of the syllogism of rules already studied under the square of opposition and conversion. The fallacy that violates this rule may be designated generically as the *fallacy of overextension.* To appreciate the need for this rule, the student should note that *the terms S and P are related to each other in the conclusion only to the extent to which they are related to M in the premises.* Thus, if either of these terms (*S* or *P*) is particular in a premise, it must remain particular in the conclusion.

> *Example:*
> MAJOR: No monkey is a man.
> MINOR: Some ambidexterous creatures are monkeys.
> CONCLUSION: No ambidexterous creatures are men.

A casual look at this example tells us that something is wrong because the conclusion states more than it should. Using our "box method" of detecting fallacies, let us put our finger on the source of the trouble.

MAJOR:	**E**	M^u	P^u
MINOR:	**I**	S^p	M^p
CONCLUSION:	**E**	S^u	P^u

Although the middle term is distributed in the major premise (and hence Rule 2 is observed), we note the *overextension* of the *S* term in the conclusion, and accordingly a violation of Rule 3. Whenever the *S* term is overextended in this fashion we have what is called a *fallacy of illicit minor*. This means simply that the minor term, *S*, is overextended in the conclusion.

> *Note:* In all instances where an illicit minor is involved (and no other fallacy) the syllogism can be validated simply by drawing a particular conclusion. In the above example we should have concluded with the **O** proposition *"Some* ambidexterous creatures are not men."

Example:
All porterhouse steaks are delicious.
No sirloin steak is a porterhouse.
No sirloin steak is delicious.

Use the box method again to test the example:

A	M^u	P^p
E	S^u	M^u
E	S^u	P^u

A glance at the results will show that the *P* term is overextended in the conclusion, in which case we have a *fallacy of illicit major*. This fallacy is so called because the major or predicate term is overextended in the conclusion.

> *Note:* It is of great practical value to know that an illicit major (overextension of *P*) can occur only in negative conclusions (**E** or **O**) because only in these instances are the predicates made universal. This does not mean, of course, that all negative conclusions contain this fallacy: only those that *overextended* the original term (P^pP^u).

EXERCISE 9.3

A. List in your notebook the names of the fallacies examined thus far in the study of the first three rules.

B. Examine the following to see if they contain any of the fallacies set forth. Before using the box method, first look for ambiguous terms. If the terms are "solid," then examine the syllogism in the way indicated above. (Assume for now that the major, minor, and conclusion appear in that order.)

   1. No soft drink is intoxicating. Some beer is intoxicating. No beer is a soft drink. (Can you correct this example?)
   2. All riots are acts of violence, and all wars are acts of violence. All wars are riots.
   3. All riots are acts of violence and some murders are not riots. Some murders are not acts of violence.
   4. Whatever is 360 degrees is hot. All circles are 360 degrees. All circles are hot.
   5. What you bought yesterday you ate today. Yesterday you bought raw fish. Today you ate raw fish.
   6. Whoever believes in the Gospel will be saved. This drowning man believes in the Gospel. This drowning man will be saved.
   7. Every freshman is inexperienced. No sophomore is a freshman. No sophomore is inexperienced.

C. Mark off the quantity of each term in the following arrangements. Decide whether there is a violation either of Rule 2 or Rule 3. If so, name the fallacy.

1. All M is P.	2. All P is M.	3. No P is M.
All M is S.	Some S is not M.	Some S is M.
All S is P.	No S is P.	Some S is not P.

4. Not all M is P.	5. All M is P.
All S is M.	Some S is not M.
No S is P.	Some S is not P.

Rule 4: **No conclusion can be drawn from two negative premises.**

   The reason for Rule 4 is simple. If both premises are negative, S and P are both *excluded* from the extension of the *intended* middle term. In this case there really is no middle term and hence no syllogism at all.

Example.
    No nominalist is a realist.
    Some English philosophers are not nominalists.
    Some English philosophers are not realists.

Note: The practical test for Rule 4 is the mood. If the mood shows up in any of the following combinations, Rule 4 is violated: **EE–, EO–, OE–, OO–.**

Rule 5: **Two affirmative premises require an affirmative conclusion.**

If (under the conditions specified by previous rules) two terms agree with a common third, then of necessity they agree with each other. This means that if *P* is *M* and if *S* likewise is *M,* then it follows that *S* is *P* and that the conclusion is therefore *affirmative.* Thus it would be wrong to reason as follows:

    Meat is good for the diet.
    Some edible items are meat.
    Some edible items are *not* good for the diet.

The conclusion here should obviously be affirmative.

Note: The practical import of Rule 5 is to know that any combination of the following will lead to an affirmative conclusion: **AA–, AI–, IA–.**

Rule 6: **A negative premise requires a negative conclusion.**

If one of the terms agrees with *M* and the other disagrees, we can only conclude that *S* and *P* must *disagree* with each other. Given the two following premises:

    No water is dry.
    Some liquid is water.

One has no choice but to conclude that

    Some liquid is *not* dry.

Note: According to the rule, any of the following combinations will require a negative conclusion: **AE–, AO–, EA–, EI–, OA–.**

General Comment. There are no special names of fallacies in violation of Rules 4, 5, and 6. If a violation occurs, simply cite the rule that is violated.

COROLLARIES

In addition to studying the rules, we should give some attention to the two following corollaries:

> 1. *No conclusion can be drawn from two particu-*
> *lar premises.*
> 2. *If one premise is particular, the conclusion must*
> *be particular.*

These corollaries are merely *specific applications* of requirements already set forth by Rules 2 and 3 of the syllogism. *They do not really add anything to the rules,* and for this reason we do not include them in our list. Yet they do serve a practical purpose. The violation of one of these corollaries is an immediate indication of the presence of one of the three following fallacies: *the fallacy of the undistributed middle, the fallacy of the illicit minor, and the fallacy of the illicit major.*

EXERCISE 9.4

On the basis of your knowledge either of the corollaries or of the rules, decide which conclusion, if any, is likely to derive from the following moods:

1. **EI–**.
2. **AI–**.
3. **AO–**.
4. **IA–**.
5. **OA–**.

VALID MOODS

Having seen both the rules and the corollaries of the syllogism, we must now discover the number of possible moods. If we restrict ourselves to premise combinations alone, we get sixteen possible moods.

AA	EA	IA	OA
AE	EE*	IE	OE*
AI	EI	II*	OI*
AO	EO*	IO*	OO*

Next we must find out how many of these moods are valid. The moods marked by an asterisk (*) are invalid because they stand for either *two negative premises* (see Rule 4) or *two particular premises* (see Corollary 1). The mood **OO** is invalid on both counts. The invalidity of the **IE** mood (not marked by an asterisk) is not quite so apparent. Note first that the *major* premise is an **I** proposition. This means that the P term, whether it appears as subject or predicate of the major premise, is *particular* (P^p). However, since the minor premise (**E**) is negative, the conclusion must be negative. Since this is so, the P term in the conclusion would be universal (P^u). Any attempt, therefore, to use an **IE** mood would result in a fallacy of *illicit major* (Rule 3).

By the process of elimination the following *eight* valid moods remain:

AA   **EA**   **IA**   **OA**
EA
AI   **EI**
AO

It cannot be assumed, however, that all of these eight remaining moods are *always* valid, for the figures in which they appear must be taken into account. In other words, we should not conclude that whenever a syllogism is in one of the above eight moods, it is automatically valid. The point of our present inquiry is simply to indicate that if a syllogism is to have any chance at all of being valid, it must fall within one of these moods.

Allowing, then, that various combinations of moods are valid for each of the four figures, we want to determine now which ones are valid and which are not. At this point various matters of practical importance must be brought to mind. First, let us raise and answer certain questions that are of value for students who are working with the syllogism for the first time.

1. HOW DO I KNOW WHICH KIND OF CONCLUSION TO DRAW? Suppose you have a "double **A** mood" (**AA**), your conclusion will have to be affirmative. If both "premises" are negative and/or particular, like an **O,** then your conclusion must be either negative or particular or both.

2. HOW DO I KNOW WHERE TO FIND THE CONCLUSION? Usually the conclusion is the last statement, but in any case it is the only statement that combines the S and P terms; it is often preceded by such words as "so" and "therefore."

3. WHICH MOODS ARE VALID FOR WHICH FIGURES? Recall that from the standpoint of premise arrangements (**AA, AE,** etc.) only eight moods

stand a chance of being valid. This does *not* mean, however, that each of these moods is valid for each of the figures in which it is cast. To decide this question you are required to work out the answers inductively—on a step-by-step basis.

DETERMINING VALIDITY

We already know how to determine the validity of a syllogism, but much further practice is needed. Accordingly, you should work with the following examples to see which are valid and which are not. If the syllogism is invalid, tell why; if not, specify its figure and its mood.

> *Note:* In some instances we shall depart from the usual order of major, minor, and conclusion. Even if the conclusion appears in another order (let us say, as the very first statement), know that this statement is what you are trying to establish. The conclusion is the "point" or purpose of the argument ("so," "therefore," and the like), and the premises are the means ("because," "since," "for," and the like).

EXERCISE 9.5

A. Determine whether the following are valid and give reasons.

1. Philosophy is a liberal art and so is literature; so they both must be the same thing.
2. All artists have fine sensibilities, but [often indicating the minor] some athletes do not. So the conclusion is obvious: no athletes have fine sensibilities.
3. Some wars are nonsensical. If you ask me why, I would say: Everything that causes useless destruction is nonsensical, and some wars do just that (cause useless destruction).
4. The desert is good for arthritis, and there's no doubt that much of Arizona is desert. So much of Arizona is good for arthritis.
5. All fish can swim and all fish have cold blood. So everything that has cold blood can swim.
6. All public parks are for enjoyment. No museum is a public park. So no museum is for enjoyment.
7. All artists are not singers. No one in our family is an artist. So no one in our family is a singer.
8. No novel is an essay and no essay is a textbook. So no textbook is a novel.

9. All men are basically equal, and all who are basically equal are the same. So all men are the same.

10. All mice like cheese. No man is a mouse. So no man likes cheese.

USING VENN DIAGRAMS

It has often been said that there is more than one way of skinning a cat, and the same holds true for testing the validity of syllogisms. We have already seen how the validity of syllogisms may be tested according to the "box method" as described in this chapter. However, there are other methods, and one of the most convenient is the use of Venn diagrams—as we shall presently see. Be it noted here that the use of these diagrams does not specifically lay bare the exact nature of the fallacy involved, if any; yet it is an altogether reliable method of determining by means of circles (a highly visual means) whether a syllogism is valid or not. A little practice will enable you to use the Venn Diagrams as a check against the box method.

> *Note:* You may wish at this point to review our previous use of Venn diagrams in Chapter 3. Our purpose there was to see the relationship *within* a proposition of terms to each other. Here we want to see the relationship of terms (*S, P,* and *M*) to each other as parts, not of a single proposition, but of the syllogism taken as a whole.

To test syllogisms by means of Venn diagrams, we shall make use of three overlapping circles. Diagram 9.1 represents what the separate sections of these overlapping circles entail.

The first section ($S\overline{P}\overline{M}$) represents only those *S*'s which are not *P*'s and not *M*'s.[4] The second section represents those *S*'s which are *P*'s but not

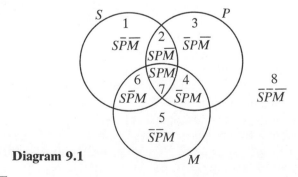

Diagram 9.1

---

[4] In all instances where the bar sign (⁻) appears above one of the terms, it is used as a sign of exclusion.

M's. In the third section we have those *P*'s which are neither *S*'s nor *M*'s. In the fourth section we have those *P*'s which are *M*'s but not *S*'s. The fifth section represents those *M*'s which are neither *S*'s nor *P*'s. The sixth section represents those *M*'s which are *S*'s but not *P*'s. In the seventh section we find those *S*'s which are both *P*'s and *M*'s. And finally, in the eighth section we find everything that is not *S*'s or *P*'s or *M*'s. In this sense the above diagram is a complete representation of our universe of discourse.

Suppose that we wanted to test (find out) the validity of the syllogism:

> All lovers of sugar are sweet.
> All flies are lovers of sugar.
> Thus, all flies are sweet.

If we let *F* represent the class of flies, *L* the class of lovers of sugar, and *S* the class of sweet things, then we can represent these three classes of things respectively, in Diagram 9.2. In order to check if the given syllogism is

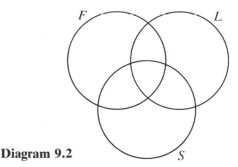

Diagram 9.2

valid, we simply diagram the major and minor premises. *We do not diagram the conclusion:* if the syllogism is valid, the conclusion will be implicitly contained in the premises; if it is not valid, the conclusion will not be contained in the premises. Thus, if the given syllogism is valid, then by diagraming the premises, we are also implicitly diagraming the conclusion. If it is invalid, then the conclusion does not appear. All we have to do in order to find out if the given syllogism is valid, therefore, is to diagram the premises. Then we check to see if the conclusion is also diagramed. If it is, the syllogism is valid; if it is not, the syllogism is invalid.

As we diagram the premises, we consider two classes for each premise. Thus the major premise, "All lovers of sugar are sweet," is represented in Diagram 9.3. The minor premise, "All flies are lovers of sugar," is represented in Diagram 9.4. Putting the two previous diagrams together, we get Diagram 9.5. We then check to see if the conclusion has been diagramed.

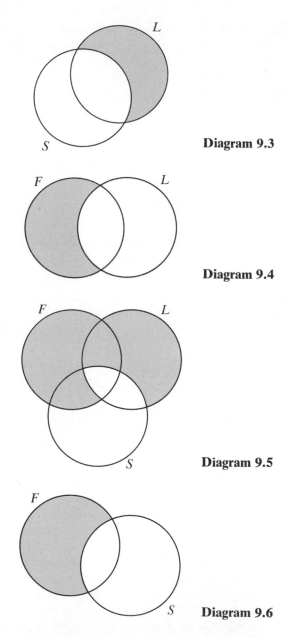

Diagram 9.3

Diagram 9.4

Diagram 9.5

Diagram 9.6

The conclusion is: "All flies are sweet." Its diagrammatic representation is shown in Diagram 9.6. Looking at the preceding diagram, we see that the conclusion has been diagramed, leading to the conclusion that the syllogism is valid. The mood of the above syllogism was **AAA,** and its figure was *1*.

In Chapter 3 we noted that the question of the truth or falsity of a categorical proposition does not arise unless there are members of the class of which we predicate something. To make this point, when we diagramed an **A** or an **E** proposition, we placed an *"x"* in the appropriate place. Thus the proposition "All satellites are man-made" was represented as Diagram 9.7.

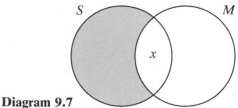

Diagram 9.7

However, in the present section we omitted the "x" in diagraming the **A** proposition in order to bring out the effectiveness of what logicians call the *hypothetical viewpoint*. According to this viewpoint, when diagraming the **A** or **E** propositions, the question of the existence of the respective members of the classes is left open. In other words, in diagrams of **A** or **E** propositions the existence of what the subject refers to need not be assumed in order to determine their truth value. Thus, from the *categorical* viewpoint we determine the truth value of the proposition "All satellites are man-made" only if there are satellites. From this point of view it is therefore understood that there are satellites. From the *hypothetical* viewpoint we simply say that *if* there are satellites, then they are all man-made. Whether there are any satellites or not is left open. We can see the distinction by examining the proposition "All satellites are man-made" from the two respective viewpoints in terms of Venn Diagrams. The two diagrams are shown in Diagram 9.8.

The adoption of either one of these viewpoints has both advantages and disadvantages. The advantage of the categorical viewpoint is that its adoption preserves all the relationships of opposition (contradictories, contraries, subcontraries and subalterns). On the other hand, if we adopt the

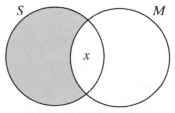

Existential Viewpoint

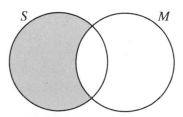

Hypothetical Viewpoint

Diagram 9.8

hypothetical viewpoint, the only relationship of opposition that we retain is that between contradictories. The reason for this is that we do not assume the existence of members of a class with respect to the **A** and **E** propositions; only the **I** and **O** propositions assert that at least one member exists. Thus we can see that subalternation, for example, does not hold. From "All *S* is *P*" we cannot infer that "Some *S* is *P*."

The main advantage of adopting the hypothetical viewpoint is that, when dealing with the **A** and **E** propositions, we do not have to commit ourselves to the existence or nonexistence of the members of their respective classes. Thus we could never commit the *existential fallacy* if we adopt this point of view—that is, we could never get into the position of predicating about nonexistent subjects.[5] In what follows we shall adopt the hypothetical viewpoint in order to see how it works. Thus with respect to the **A** and **E** propositions, the existence of the subject will be left open (as already explained), while the **I** and **O** propositions will be understood as saying that at least one member exists.

Suppose that we wanted to find out whether the validity of the syllogism

> Some mice are not white.
> All mice are recalcitrant.
> Thus some recalcitrant things are not white.

Diagraming the two premises, we get Diagram 9.9. If we check the conclusion, we see that it has been diagramed simultaneously with the two premises. The *"x"* represents at least one recalcitrant thing which is not

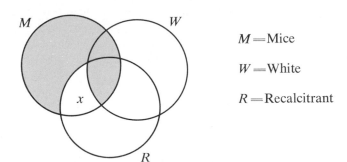

M = Mice

W = White

R = Recalcitrant

Diagram 9.9

---

[5] It must also be understood that this does not imply that by adopting the existential viewpoint we *do* get into this predicament. From the existential viewpoint, we cannot determine the truth value of a proposition in the first place, *unless* members of the class about which we are predicating, *do exist.* If they do not exist, then the whole question of truth or falsity is irrelevant.

white; therefore the syllogism is valid. Also note that this example clarifies an important point: in diagraming the premises, *always diagram the universal premise first.* The reason is that otherwise it becomes difficult to know where to place the *"x"* of any particular premise. The diagram was worked out in the steps shown in Diagram 9.10.

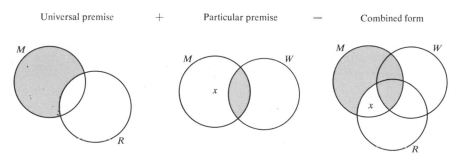

Diagram 9.10

Let us now test the following syllogism in order to find out whether it is valid:

All whales are good swimmers.
All good swimmers are muscular.
So, some whales are muscular.

Letting *W* stand for whales, *G* for good swimmers, and *M* for muscular, we diagram the preceding argument (syllogism) in Diagram 9.11.

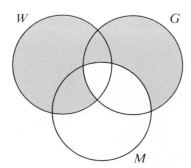

Diagram 9.11

If you examine the diagraming of the two premises closely, you will see that the conclusion is not contained in them. The syllogism is therefore invalid. It is invalid because we have made an inference from two universal premises to a particular one. Since the universal premises leave the question of the existence of the subject open, we cannot infer a particular premise from them. Particular premises are understood as asserting the existence of at least one member of the class in question. In the above syllogism the existential fallacy has been committed, thus invalidating the argument.

An unusual syllogism is the following:

> Some peaches are not fuzzy.
> Some fuzzy things are not delicious.
> Therefore, some peaches are not delicious.

Letting P stand for peaches, F for fuzzy, and D for delicious, we diagram the two premises of the above syllogism in Diagram 9.12. In diagraming the first premise of the above syllogism, we place an "x" in that part of the P circle which is independent of the F circle. But if we look closely, we see that the area in question is made up of two sections—1 and 6. Since those

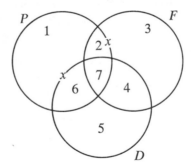

Diagram 9.12

peaches which are not fuzzy could be in either one of those sections, we simply place an "x" on the line which joins them. The same procedure applies to the second premise. Since those fuzzy things which are not delicious could be in either section 2 or section 3, we place an "x" on the line joining those two sections. Looking at the conclusion, we see that it has not been diagramed explicitly. If the "x" were explicitly in section 1, then our syllogism would be valid. But since we do not know whether it is in section 1 or 6, the syllogism is invalid.

EXERCISE 9.6

A. By means of Venn diagrams, determine whether the following syllogisms are valid or invalid:

1. All burglars are sneaky.
    No burglars are lazy.
    So no sneaky people are lazy.
2. All salamanders are green.
    Some frogs are green.
    Therefore, some salamanders are frogs.
3. No man is an island.
    No island is a peninsula.
    No man is a peninsula.
4. Some reticulated wire is rusty.
    All reticulated wire is pungent.
    So, some pungent things are rusty.
5. Some Ferraris are not red.
    Some red things are not speedy.
    Thus some Ferraris are not speedy.
6. All unicorns are fighters of dragons.
    All fighters of dragons are fearful of fire.
    Thus all unicorns are fearful of fire.
7. All fighters of dragons are fearful of fire.
    All unicorns are fighters of fire.
    Some unicorns are fearful of fire.
8. Every pernicious witch is a lover of mischief.
    Penelope is a lover of mischief.
    So Penelope must be a pernicious witch.
9. All Gila monsters are lovers of the desert sun.
    Some lovers of the desert sun are cacti.
    So some Gila monsters are cacti.
10. All big boats in the little lake are little boats in the big lake.
    This is a little boat in a big lake.
    So this must be a big boat in a little lake.

B. With respect to all those syllogisms above which are invalid, name the fallacy involved.

chapter 10

Argumentative Discourse

Enthymemes as Probable Arguments
Sign Arguments
The Enthymeme as Abbreviated Syllogism
How to Supply Missing Parts
Logical Puzzlers
Chain Arguments

Our study of the basic theory of the syllogism leaves open the question of how to relate this theory to everyday argumentative discourse. It is the purpose of this chapter to provide the basic means for accomplishing this objective.

ENTHYMEMES AS PROBABLE ARGUMENTS

Generally speaking, an enthymeme is an abbreviated form of argument in which the major premise, minor premise, or conclusion is implied; this we shall take up in a later section of this chapter. Our first concern, however, is to examine the enthymeme in its original meaning—as a type of argument that suppresses its major premise. According to this traditional view, the reason for suppressing the major is that it involves some kind of statement most persons could agree upon, even though the basis of agreement is only probable and nonscientific. Suppose we say that Smith hates Jones *because* he is envious of him. This syllogism (whose major premise is implied) rests on the assumption which is *probably* true and *generally accepted* that

Men hate those of whom they are envious.

In the sense just described, many categorical arguments are enthymemes because they fall far short of the ideal, in which the major premise possesses a high degree of necessity. Arguments of this sort, even though they are deductive, have only probable weight because the major premise rests on a somewhat shaky foundation and hardly measures up to the requirement of an **A** or **E** proposition as defined in Chapter 5.

How, then, are we to regard arguments of this sort? Shall we reject them out of hand on the grounds that they lack the degree of certainty that is required for a strictly deductive type of argument? Or shall we allow that they do have a value of their own?

> *Example:*
> Americans are activistically inclined.
> Since you are an American,
> You too are activistically inclined.

Arguments like the one in the example do have a limited practical value, provided we avoid the temptation of drawing a necessary conclusion where no strictly logical necessity exists.[1] In other words,

> *If one or more of the premises of a syllogism has*
> *no more than a probable value, then the conclu-*
> *sion itself is only* probably *true.*

While most argumentation is of a nonscientific nature, we should be wrong on that account to consider it worthless. Thus, *even though we may reason from premises that are only probably true, the conclusions we arrive at are frequently of the utmost practical value.* The reasoning, for instance, that enters into the making of a foreign-policy decision is nonscientific. Yet in the consequences that such a decision involves, the reasoning employed is of paramount practical value.

From the discussion of the original and still valid meaning of the term "enthymeme" taken as a probable argument an important practical consideration comes to the fore:

> *Whenever you examine an argument, examine it*
> *carefully for any hidden assumptions or premises*
> *it may contain.*

More will be said on this point as this chapter continues, but let us note now that there is no more important aspect of logic as critical thinking than that of filling out the missing parts, assumptions, and premises of an argument.

---

[1] That is, no logical necessity exists in terms of the *truth value,* not the validity, of the argument as a whole. As to the *validity* of such arguments, provided they measure up to the formal requirements of the syllogism, they are as valid as any other.

EXERCISE 10.1

Informally state what you consider the hidden assumption of each of the following arguments:

1. Your school must be one of the finest in the Midwest. I know of none that has a better basketball team.
2. None of us knows what it is really like to die because we've never had the experience of dying.
3. This man must have heart trouble because he has all the known symptoms of heart disease.
4. You'll probably pass all your courses because you're the smartest guy in the class.
5. It's doubtful that the President will be reelected. He's lost his appeal to the workers.

No doubt you have had little difficulty in working out the above exercises—they are very simple. To that extent, however, you have "gotten your feet wet" in what will turn out to be one of the most important sections in your study of logic—the enthymeme. But there is another very practical suggestion: whether you are dealing with enthymemes or any other type of argument, do not be unreasonable in expecting a higher degree of certainty than the argument itself is capable of delivering.

As noted above, it is wrong to think that probable arguments are useless on the grounds that they do not conform to rigid a priori standards of certainty. Knowledge of whatever sort is a human property, and it must be made to serve human purposes. It is important, then, not to make all of our reasoning conform, let us say, to a strictly mathematical mold but to adjust ourselves to the nature of the subject we are examining. It is within such a context that the strength or weakness of an argument should be judged.

EXERCISE 10.2

In the light of the above remarks, evaluate the following statement:

Either you know something to be true or not. If you know it, then you are certain of it, otherwise you are in a state of ignorance or doubt. Either way there is nothing that is only *probably* true.

SIGN ARGUMENTS

Critical thinking requires us to know when to judge from signs. As a matter of fact, enthymemes are often regarded as arguments from a sign. Thus, it is "argued" from the redness of a person's cheeks that he is shy or embarrassed; from the cloudiness of the sky that it will rain; from the un-couthness of a person's appearance that he is uncultured; from the discolor of a piece of meat that it is old; from the hardness of a loaf of bread that it is stale. Examples of this kind can be multiplied indefinitely. From the few here given it should be clear that much of our everyday "reasoning" is of this kind. Under ordinary circumstances the argument from a sign leads to no necessary conclusion, and the *failure to take this into account is the source of an incredible number of mistakes which people commit in their everyday life.*[2] At their best most sign arguments only provide a *clue* to a problem which must be solved by the use of induction, and induction is not a simple matter of inference at all.

A few further words should be said about an argument from a sign, if only to anticipate subsequent treatment of induction. First we should be careful not to attribute to signs any more than their natural worth. A human footprint in the sand is, of course, an indication that *someone* had been there; but we should not be too quick to judge that the footprint in question is that of the very person we are looking for.

Let us say, then, that it is part of the business of logic to put us on guard against a too heavy reliance on the argument from a sign. Normally we have to depend upon signs and symptoms as clues to a problem that has to be solved, as when a doctor diagnoses a patient. Yet we should not com-mit the fallacy either of the chronic optimist or of the chronic pessimist who hastily interprets a given sign as an indication of either perfect health or fatal disease. The important thing—in the interpretation of signs—is to reserve judgment until further evidence can be had.

EXERCISE 10.3

Respond to the following.

1. Discuss the problems of the hypochondriac in his reliance on the argument from a sign.
2. Show how gossips are particularly susceptible to "arguments" from a sign.

---

[2] This is especially true if the sign argument in question is based merely on a *conventional* sign. Thus, it is fallacious to think that because the term "invaluable" contains the prefix "in," the term in question means *"not valuable."* If, on the other hand, a sign argument is based on a *natural sign,* there is perhaps less likelihood of going astray, although here, too, the sign should be taken only as a clue for a prob-lem that is to be solved on its own merits by means of induction—that is, by further observation, hypothesis, and the experimental testing of hypotheses. Thus, gray hair is *under certain conditions* a sign of advancing age; a cloudy sky is *under certain con-ditions* a sign of rain; a persistent cough is *under certain conditions* a sign of tuber-culosis.

3. Name some of the signs by which professors sometimes judge students to be irresponsible in their work.

4. Sometimes a bloodstain on the floor is taken to be the sign of a murder. Give instances in which the use of such signs is often false or misleading.

5. Provide further instances of arguments and of cases that are too hastily drawn up from signs.

THE ENTHYMEME AS ABBREVIATED SYLLOGISM

We have examined the meaning of enthymemes as probable arguments and as arguments from a sign. We must finally consider the most general use of the enthymeme in its reference to *any* kind of argument in which one of the parts is missing. Applied to the categorical syllogism, this means that

> *an enthymeme is an abbreviated syllogism that*
> *implies either one of its premises or it conclu-*
> *sion.*

We encounter such enthymemes frequently in everyday life, since it seldom happens that we find a neat, full-fledged syllogism, with a conveniently arranged major, minor, and conclusion. A reader would be surprised if he read in the editorial of his evening newspaper:

> No incompetent official is deserving of reelection.
> Mr. Willoughby is an incompetent official.
> Therefore, Mr. Willoughby is not deserving of reelection.

More probably the same line of argument (with considerable rhetorical fill-in) would be expressed in one of the following ways:

> Being an incompetent official, Mr. Willoughby does not deserve to be reelected.

> Incompetent officials are hardly deserving of reelection. Mr. Willoughby should be rejected at the polls.

> Incompetence in office is hardly a brief for reelection. Is there anyone in this community who has a reasonable doubt as to the incompetence of that scoundrel, Mr. Willoughby?

At first glance these three statements seem a far cry from the syllogism as studied in the last few chapters. Yet, in spite of their verbal dissimilarity, each of these statements is *logically identical* with the syllogism presented before.

Let us begin, then, to penetrate the rhetorical word combinations of common parlance to reach an understanding of the basic skeleton of the argument. Note that the logical structure of the above enthymemes is as follows:

1. Suppressed major.
   S is *M*.
   S is not *P*.

2. No *M* is *P*.
   Suppressed minor.
   S is not *P*.

3. No *M* is *P*.
   S is *M*.
   Suppressed conclusion.

For purposes of convenience, syllogisms with a suppressed major, minor, or conclusion are designated as enthymemes of the *first, second,* or *third* order, respectively.

HOW TO SUPPLY MISSING PARTS

Arguments with Missing Conclusions

Since there is no magic formula by which to supply the missing parts of arguments, we shall have to restrict ourselves to a few practical suggestions and let the good judgment of the reader do the rest. As a start, recall the importance of knowing, in the first place, precisely *what the argument is intended to prove.* The first thing to do, therefore, is to *set forth the conclusion.*

If the conclusion is given, there is very little difficulty in locating it, since it is usually preceded by such words or phrases as "hence," "therefore," "consequently," "as a result," and "it follows that." Even if the conclusion is suppressed (third-order enthymeme), one can readily supply it by simply determining the *point* of the argument in question. Recall again that the premises are only the means for *pointing to* the conclusion—the conclusion being the end or reason for which anything else appears in an argument.

EXERCISE 10.4

In the following examples supply the missing conclusion. Remember again that the conclusion contains the *S* and *P* terms, and that the middle term never appears in the conclusion.

1. No good novelist is a poor writer. But some good novelists are Americans. Ergo?
2. Musical comedies are light-hearted dramatizations. But no Shakespearean tragedy is a musical comedy.
3. All the world's great philosophers were geniuses, and every genius is endowed with a high IQ.
4. All medical students are potential doctors, and no potential doctor is a practicing physician.
5. All people who snore should sleep in an isolated section of the house. But my brother is the world's champion snorer.

Only a casual inspection of the above statements should convince the reader of the comparative ease in dealing with third-order enthymemes. Viewing these examples will also help him to understand why it is generally considered polite to let people draw their own conclusions: to do anything less is frequently an insult to the listener's intelligence.

Arguments with Missing Premises

We have already spoken of the importance of supplying hidden assumptions in an argument. The problem consists of supplying a missing major in a first-order enthymeme and a missing minor premise in second-order enthymemes. In all such instances, however, it is important first to set forth the conclusion of the argument. Recall again that the conclusion of the argument is its point or purpose, the premises being the means or the reason given in defense of the conclusion.

EXERCISE 10.5

As a preliminary exercise, determine which part of the argument in the following examples is the conclusion, which the premise. To complete this exercise reread if necessary the paragraph above.

1. Because you are a registered Democrat, you will, I am sure, vote Democratic.

2. Some doctors' fees are unjust because the doctors rob you blind.

3. A good football player needs a lot of training because a good football player has to be fast on his feet.

4. Because Kennedy was a popular president, his death was greatly mourned by the people.

5. Good men deserve a reward, and therefore you deserve one too.

Only in the last of the above statements did the word "therefore" appear as a clue to the conclusion. However, it is doubtful that you had any serious difficulty in determining the point of the above arguments even without such words as "therefore," whether the conclusion was maintained in its usual last place or not.

As for supplying the missing premise of an argument, keep in mind that once you have your conclusion, you already know your S and P terms. Accordingly, if the premise that is given contains the S term, you know that your minor is given.

Example:

$$S \qquad\qquad P \qquad\qquad S$$

Some *congressmen* should be *voted out of office* because *they* are
$$M$$
dishonest.

Our example is a first-order enthymeme because the major is missing. Obviously the supplied major will have to be an affirmative statement (since the conclusion is affirmative), and it will also have to be universal (no conclusion is possible from *two* particular premises). As we link up M and P we have a choice, then, of the following:

$$M \qquad\qquad\qquad P$$
1. All *dishonest men* should be *voted out of office.*

or

$$P \qquad\qquad\qquad M$$
2. All *men who should be voted out of office* are *dishonest men.*

Apart from the fact that the latter statement happens to be false, it would, if we used it, lead to an undistributed middle. Let us therefore reconstruct our syllogism by using the first:

SUPPLIED MAJOR: All dishonest men should be voted out of office.
MINOR: Some congressmen are dishonest.

CONCLUSION: Some congressmen should be voted out of office.

The syllogism as it now stands is complete and valid.

As we work out examples of this sort, we should try to reconstruct them in ways that validate them. However, if an argument turns out to be invalid in spite of any attempt to correct it, we are correct in thinking that the argument was invalid from the outset.

Another example contains a negative conclusion:

> Some newspapers are not worth reading.
> No sensational newspaper is worth reading.

Offhand you may be confused here as to which part of the enthymeme is the conclusion. If so, resolve your doubt by noting that the second statement backs up the first and is therefore given, however implicitly, as the *reason* for the first. The first statement should therefore be taken as the conclusion. If you can immediately supply the missing premise, do so without further delay.

It is the minor that is missing in the example, since the P term is given in the conclusion. The supplied minor should therefore read in one of two ways:

$$S \qquad\qquad M$$
1. Some newspapers are sensational.

or

$$M \qquad\qquad S$$
2. Some sensational things are newspapers.

Since (1) is much more natural than (2), let us restate our syllogism as follows:

> MAJOR: No sensational newspaper is worth reading.
> SUPPLIED MINOR: Some newspapers are sensational.
> CONCLUSION: Some newspapers are not worth reading.

The syllogism as it stands is an **EIO** in Figure 1, and it is valid. However, in practical argumentation we might want to test the premises; we might want to know further why sensational newspapers are not worth reading, what is meant by "sensational," and which newspapers are sensational and which are not, and so on.

EXERCISE 10.6

Supply the missing premise as needed and whenever possible make statements that are true. Determine whether the enthymeme is first or second order.

1. All men deserve to be treated as men, and so criminals deserve to be treated as men.
2. Your foreign policy is misguided because it's based on the premise that you can dominate the world.
3. Beethoven's works will never lose their appeal. *No* great masterpiece ever loses its appeal.
4. This argument is an enthymeme because one of its parts is missing.
5. This ship has a low ceiling height. All oriental ships do.
6. It's no fun shopping downtown because there's no place to park.
7. Not everyone is capable of making a trip to the moon because traveling to the moon means going through outer space.
8. According to Aristotle, being temperate means living according to the "golden mean." This implies that very few people are temperate.
9. No man-made problem is irreversible in its effects. Therefore air pollution is not irreversible.
10. "Being a car salesman, you are probably a liar."

LOGICAL PUZZLERS

A further examination of arguments in their everyday dress reveals that they are seldom reducible to a simple logical form. At this point, therefore, the reader is asked to use his understanding of the syllogism, not as a kind of rigid logical straitjacket, but as a guideline to arguments that often represent in varying degrees a departure from the norm. Frequently, too, many words and expressions as they appear in argumentation and debate have no more than a rhetorical value, and it is part of the business of practical logic to separate the wheat from the chaff; this is largely done by common sense—which is seldom as common as it is supposed to be; much practice is therefore needed.

In any attempt to evaluate categorical arguments one should, of course, use the basic rules of the syllogism as the guidelines of critical thought. Yet in combination with the rules he should also keep in mind the practical importance of the following suggestions:

1. EXAMINE ARGUMENTS FOR THE STEADINESS AND CONSISTENCY OF THEIR TERMS. In effect such examination puts to use Rule 1—that is, the rule which forbids the use of ambiguous or equivocal terms.

2. LOOK FOR SELF-CONTRADICTORY PREMISES. Occasionally people contradict themselves in the very course of one and the same argument; here again it is therefore important to be on one's guard. (See Chapter 3 on "self-contradictory premises.")

3. MAKE EXPLICIT THE HIDDEN ASSUMPTIONS THAT ANY ARGUMENT MAY CONTAIN.

Examples:

Most of the following examples represent a departure from the norm. They are not the neat type of syllogisms that we have been presenting so far, and the reason for studying them is to understand the many variations of the categorical syllogism, and to learn how to handle syllogisms in a more freewheeling fashion than we have done so far.

1. This Japanese ship will be open for inspection in our harbor today because today is Sunday, and every Sunday is a day for viewing foreign ships.

> *Explanation:* An attempt to reduce this example to a single syllogism will lead to frustration. However, we should note the assumption that "This (Japanese) ship *is* a foreign ship." Fully set forth, the argument would read: Every Sunday is a day for viewing foreign ships; today is Sunday; today *is* a day for viewing foreign ships. This Japanese (frigate) is a foreign ship, so it too may be viewed today.

2. Only the mayor will be admitted to the meeting because this meeting is intended for civic officials alone.

> *Explanation:* The obvious assumption here is that the mayor is a civic official, and the meaning of "only" will have to be gathered from the context so as to exclude non-civic officials, whoever they may be. The basic syllogism: All civic officials may attend; the mayor is a civic official (and the only one); the mayor may attend.

3. Only women are mothers. Men are not women. So men are not mothers.

> *Explanation:* If we restrict ourselves here only to a formal application of the rules, we should have to say that we have an illicit major. However, the unique function of "only" in the major premise serves to distribute the major term "mothers"; the syllogism as it stands is therefore really a valid argument.

4. Anyone except a moron would pass this test. Pogo is a moron.

> *Explanation:* The conclusion here is that Pogo will not pass the test. Though two affirmative statements normally take an affirmative conclusion, the effect of the major is to say in context: No moron

will pass this test. Given this to be so, it will follow that Pogo will not pass.

5. Every official *as such* is deserving of respect. This dishonest politician *is* an official.

Explanation: The major of this argument is what logicians call a "reduplicative statement," since it calls special attention to the manner in which the predicate is ascribed to the subject. However, since the minor premise seems to ignore the qualification introduced in the major, we have in effect an ambiguous middle term. Therefore, it does not follow that this dishonest politician deserves respect except in the original sense.

6. Only one person will win the prize. Since I am only one person, I shall win.

Explanation: Here we have another instance of an ambiguous middle. In examples of this sort the student should not only recognize the ambiguity but also analyze its source. Here the phrase "only one person" is taken indeterminately in the major; in the minor it is taken in a definite, or determinate, sense.

7. Putting people into categories is a dangerous game. But logic teaches us how to do just that. So logic teaches us a dangerous game.

Explanation: Another instance of an ambiguous middle: it all depends on how and under what conditions you "put people into categories."

EXERCISE 10.7

In a manner similar to what we have done above, analyze the following examples. In the case of enthymemes, supply what is missing.

1. All students except freshmen have privileges, and it seems that for one whole year I'm condemned to the life of a freshman. Ergo, I shall not have any privileges. (Why a negative conclusion?)
2. Only psychiatrists can save a world that has gone mad, and the whole world *has* gone mad. (Draw the conclusion and point up any inconsistencies, assumptions, and the like, contained in the premises).
3. No one can believe a philosopher because philosophers are always contradicting each other. (Specify the hidden premise and examine it for its truth value.)
4. Men as such are rational beings. But no statement that I know of is more contradictory to my experience. So there must be something wrong with the intended conclusion that you are rational *because* you're a man.

CHAIN ARGUMENTS

We have noted that an argument may contain, not merely one, but an entire series of syllogisms. Arguments of this sort are known as polysyllogism ("poly-" meaning "many"). In its most ordinary sense, a polysyllogism is taken to mean a series of syllogisms that are so connected that the conclusion of one "doubles" as a premise (usually as the *major* premise) for the one that follows. Thus:

> Anything that has life has a soul.
> All things that breathe have life.
> *All things that breathe have a soul.   (*Conclusion 1*)
> Every animal is a thing that breathes.
> *Every animal has a soul.   (*Conclusion 2*)
> Man is an animal.
> *Man has a soul.   (*Conclusion 3*)
> John is a man.
> John has a soul.   (*Conclusion 4*)

In the above argument each conclusion marked by an asterisk (*) serves as the major premise for the syllogism that follows.

A special form of polysyllogism is the *sorites*. This latter is a chain argument in which all the conclusions are suppressed *except the last*. The Aristotelian sorites is the best known form; and it may be symbolized as shown in Diagram 10.1.

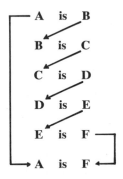

Diagram 10.1

This type of argument is identified by noting that

   1. the predicate of each premise functions as the subject of the one that follows;

2. the subject of the conclusion is the subject of the original premise, and the predicate of the conclusion is the predicate of the premise that preceded it.

In dealing with any polysyllogism, one must be especially careful to avoid ambiguity in the use of terms, as is illustrated by the following sorites:

Whatever is *likely* is probable.
Whatever is probable is uncertain.
Whatever is uncertain is unknown.
Whatever is unknown is unpredictable.
Whatever is unpredictable is *impossible to guess.*
Whatever is *likely* is *impossible to guess.*

In this argument there is considerable ambiguity in the use of such terms as "uncertain," "unknown," and "unpredictable"—terms that stand in radical need of some qualification or distinction. For example, in the statement "Whatever is unknown is unpredictable" the question arises whether something is *absolutely* unknown or only *relatively* so. The statement as it stands would be true only if something were completely (absolutely) unknown. One must always be prepared to make distinctions of this sort, especially in the use of "chain" argument.

EXERCISE 10.8

Examine the following multiple arguments for their validity, and set forth, if necessary, their logical structure.

1. All who love wisely live wisely.
   All happily married persons love wisely.
   All happily married persons live wisely.
   Some men are not happily married.
   Some men do not live wisely.
2. No cat is a dog.
   All German shepherds are dogs.
   No German shepherd is a cat.
   Some German shepherds are herdsmen.
   Some herdsmen are cats.
   (This example contains two fallacies. Try to locate both of them.)
3. All peace-loving persons hate war.
   No one who hates war loves violence.
   No one who loves violence is peace-loving.

All rabble rousers love violence.
So no rabble rousers are peace-loving (persons).

4. Everyone who eats gets hungry.
   Whoever gets hungry needs food.
   Whoever needs food is weak.
   Anyone who is weak is feeble.
   All who are feeble are sick.
   So anyone who eats gets sick.

5. Anyone who works gets tired.
   All who get tired need rest.
   All who need rest are sleepy.
   All who are sleepy are unfit for work.
   Anyone who works is unfit for work.

chapter 11

Practical Argumentation and How it Works

The Epicheirema: How to Expose It
A Practical Code for Debate
How to Build Up an Argument
Other Modes of Argumentation: Reductio Ad Absurdum

We have come a long way toward understanding what logic is about. In the early part of our study we emphasized the importance of a realistic approach to logic. A realistic logic is based on an understanding of the connection that exists between our mental operations and the empirical data from which they are drawn. This connection was made particularly evident in the case of the categorical syllogism, and in the past two chapters we have been working out on a technical basis the implications of such a theory. In the present chapter we shall continue along much the same lines, but with a view toward a yet more practical approach that will stress both the critical and the constructive side of logic. In the first section we shall keep our eye on various substitutes for argumentation—such as the use of image appeal—which often lead people into believing themselves to be thinking critically when in point of fact they are not.

THE EPICHEIREMA: How to Expose It

In addition to knowing what an enthymeme is and how to handle it, the reader should know that a great deal of what appears in an ordinary piece of argumentative discourse is usually of a narrative, descriptive, or expository nature. Examine for instance, the following paragraph.

> An economy that is based on excessive taxation is *fundamentally* an unsound economy. Every government has, of course, the right to tax both individuals and corporations, inasmuch as taxation is the only means that a government has of maintaining itself in existence. When, however, the costs of taxation are so high that they are prejudicial to a *free* economy, a situation has developed in which the government

is no longer serving the interests of the citizenry at large. Is there any doubt about the fact that the economy of our government (based as it is on a system of excessive taxation) is *fundamentally* an unsound economy?

In studying an argument of this sort, the reader will do well before examining any of its expository details to set forth its *leading major and minor premises* as well as its *leading conclusion*. What is the main point of the argument in question? Clearly, that

> The economy of our government is fundamentally an unsound economy.

The fact that the conclusion of the original statement is set forth in the form of a rhetorical question should in no way mislead the person who reads it into thinking that it is not a vital part of the argument. What reason, then, is given in support of this proposition, arrived at by way of conclusion? It is the assertion (parenthetically stated) that

> The economy of our government is one that is based on excessive taxation.

Syllogistically stated, then, the above argument should read:

> MAJOR: Any economy that is based on excessive taxation is fundamentally an unsound economy.
> MINOR: The economy of our government is one that is based on excessive taxation.
> CONCLUSION: The economy of our government is fundamentally an unsound economy.

Now that we have stated the argument in this form, we are in a far better position to examine it from the standpoint of both its logical structure and the truth value of its premises. We can also see that the part of the original paragraph that was not expressly set forth in our syllogism is given merely in support of the major premise.

An even more careful analysis of the example reveals that the major premise is supported by an argument of its own—that is, by an argument with respect to which the major itself might be regarded as a conclusion. This type of argument is most often referred to by logicians as an *epicheirema*.

Thus, an epicheirema is an argument that consists of *one basic syllogism*—with a leading major and minor premise—and a leading conclusion. What characterizes it, however, as a special form of argument is the fact that a *reason* is attached to one or both of its premises. The following is a clear-cut illustration of this type of syllogism.

Example:

MAJOR: Every realistic system of education is based on the needs of the student,
because the failure to cope with these needs defeats the very purpose for which education is intended.
MINOR: Some systems of education, however, are not based on the needs of the student,
because they do not include adequate programs for vocational guidance, which, clearly, is one of the student's most basic needs.
CONCLUSION: Some systems of education are not realistic.

There are, of course, various ways in which a *series* of syllogisms might be employed as part of the general fabric of an argumentative piece of discourse. However, the resolution of an argument into every *single* syllogism that is contained in it would prove not only tedious but in many respects impractical. It is suggested accordingly that, in analyzing an argument, the student devote the major share of his attention (initially at least) to an examination of the leading points of the argument.

A PRACTICAL CODE FOR DEBATE

To handle certain arguments in the manner of the above examples, you must keep in mind the importance, not of the rules (since we already studied them), but of a number of practical reminders that may well serve as guidelines in argumentation and debate. These reminders should be kept in mind whenever we evaluate an argument. Perhaps after you have studied them you may want to add more suggestions to the list; in any case, they should provide you with a variety of criteria for the practical handling of arguments in discussion and debate.

1. In studying an argument, *try to determine whether it is inductive or deductive;* in practice both methods often dovetail. Fundamentally, inductive arguments are concerned with such matters as problem solving, the framing of hypotheses, and testing; whereas deductive arguments normally proceed from more or less universal statements or rules to a particular application of them.

2. Does the person who presents the argument have a clear-cut idea

of what he wants to prove? If he has not stated his conclusion, what, in the context of his premises, is the conclusion?

3. Is it possible that the person presenting the argument is trying to prove too much? In this connection it is good to keep in mind an old Latin saying: *Qui nimis probat, nihil probat*—"He who proves too much proves nothing."

4. In the give-and-take of ordinary dialectical exchange you should get into the habit, wherever doubt exists, of asking what the speaker is trying to prove or establish. Many disagreements can often be resolved once this becomes clear; in any case it is fruitless to have a long argument where the sole point of a disagreement centers on the faulty use of terms.

5. Concerning the matter of terms, *always ask, wherever a doubt exists, what the speaker means by his terms.* Do not, however, overwork this procedure to the point of captiousness; it is simply a matter of fair play to take commonly accepted terms in their commonly accepted meanings.

6. The claim is frequently made that *all* disputes are terminological ones. *Be hesitant to accept such a universal statement;* the fact is that many arguments, contrary to nominalistic assumptions, are based on a real difference of outlook.

7. *Do not be too quick to agree with a statement if there is a solid doubt in your mind whether you can accept it or not.* Many persons are too quick to agree with arguments they do not really understand. Accordingly, the best approach is to lay bare your disagreements and misgivings wherever they exist. In effect, you should never concede what you do not understand —you may regret it later.

8. *Get to the heart of the argument.* You should ask the person who is presenting the argument to give a "nutshell" presentation of it; if he cannot do so himself, try to paraphrase it yourself—all the while asking whether your own statement is a fair presentation of his position.

9. *Examine the evidence.* Once the structure of the argument is made clear, examine the evidence upon which it rests. In the case of syllogistic reasoning, you must examine the syllogism, not only for its logical validity, but also for the truth value of the premises, especially if one of the premises is hidden or suppressed. Examination of the evidence further means that you take a close look at the middle term to see whether it actually functions as a solid and convincing reason for the assertion made in the conclusion.

10. Point out any irrelevancies, inconsistencies, and so on, that appear in the course of the argument, with a view, especially in oral discourse, toward keeping it on its main track.

11. Be on your guard against various types of appeal (to ignorance, prejudice, and the like), such as we studied in Chapter 3.

EXERCISE 11.1

Keeping in mind what you have studied in this chapter, set forth the nucleus of the following arguments. Determine also whether the arguments are valid and whether the premises are true. Be on the lookout for hidden assumptions.

1. Being a conscientious objector, you cannot be a loyal American citizen. No conscientious objector is a loyal American citizen. If you have any doubt about my argument, let me explain it. In the first place no conscientious objector is a loyal American citizen because it's perfectly obvious by a logical process of conversion that no loyal American citizen is a conscientious objector. However, if you still doubt the truth of my premise, I'll give you another argument to prove it: every loyal citizen believes in fulfilling the duty he has to his country. But conscientious objectors do not believe in fulfilling their duty because they are opposed to the draft. [Examine the hidden assumption that underlies this argument.] So it follows again that conscientious objectors are not loyal citizens, and that you, being a conscientious objector, are not loyal either.

2. I find it hard to accept your conclusion that no thief is untrustworthy, but I guess you must be right because you've taken a course in logic and you ought to know better. Let's see now, how did your argument go? Something like this, as I recall: you said that all liars are untrustworthy, and that no thief is a liar, so no thief is untrustworthy. Since I have to admit that both your premises are true, I suppose I have no way of avoiding your conclusion.

3. Bill Jones is a local contractor who should not be allowed to stay in business. I know a lot of people, including myself, who were swindled by this local contractor. In my own case, I paid him for the cost both of labor and materials for an addition to my home, and as it turned out, I later received from the lumber company a bill for the cost of the materials. Talk about cheating! No contractor who is in the habit of swindling people should be allowed to stay in business. So again, I say, let's get rid of people like Bill Jones.

4. Now that we have a majority of newly elected Republican governors, we're going to see some real progress in the states. That's what I hold, anyway, because *all* Republicans are in favor of progress, and since these newly elected officials are (all of them) "dyed-in-the-wool" Republicans, they will be progressive too. You wait and see.

5. Every time there's an increase in taxes, the purchasing power of

your dollar goes down. Every time the purchasing power of your dollar goes down, you get poorer, and every time you get poorer you have less to eat, and every time you have less to eat you are on the way to starvation. So it follows (according to this lengthy syllogism) that every time there's an increase in taxes, you're on the way to starvation.

HOW TO BUILD UP AN ARGUMENT

Structuring an argument is not as haphazard a job as many people think. In our effort, therefore, toward putting logic to creative as well as to critical use, some special attention should be given to what we have already explained in our general theory of the syllogism: for all practical intents, categorical reasoning consists of seeing how particular applications can be made of more generalized statements. As you attempt to build up an argument, therefore, keep these important points in mind:

1. Know what you want to prove;
2. Relate the object of your proof to some wider statement that you intend to use as a premise.

For example, if you want to show that some plants are hard to grow in the desert, look for a reason—such as in the fact that *all* plants that require much shade are hard to grow in the desert; if you want to prove that no whale is a fish, look for the reason in the more universal statement that no *mammal* is a fish, it being the case that all whales are mammals; if you want to prove that some politicians are dishonest, relate this more particular truth to the premise that *all* dishonest persons have little regard for justice; and so on. The point to be grasped is this: the search for premises is the search for a reason, and the reason is generally to be found in some universal statement from which the particular statement derives.

Begin, then, with a clear-cut statement of your conclusion, such as the following:

> Many of our fellow citizens are unjust in their attitude toward minority groups.

Possibly you want to build a whole series of arguments around this basic conclusion, but in the beginning decide what your basic proof will be. To do so you must inquire as to the types of evidence that are available for showing that many of your fellow citizens are unjust toward minority groups. No doubt many such evidences come to mind, such as those involving discrimination in housing, violation of civil rights as in the use of public transportation, and so on. Since your conclusion, however, is a fairly general one, you may proceed with evidence given as a middle term that is also fairly general. Thus:

> Many of our fellow citizens are unjust in their attitude toward minority groups because they are *unwilling to recognize a basic equality of rights*.

At the present stage of the argument, you have a second-order enthymeme —a conclusion together with a minor premise. Let us therefore set forth our major premise—as the wider and more universal truth in the light of which the somewhat more particular truths of the minor and conclusion are actually known. Thus:

> Anyone who is unwilling to recognize a basic equality of rights is unjust in his attitude toward minority groups.

Here we have generalized an idea that can now be put to particular use in our conclusion:

> MAJOR: Anyone who is unwilling to recognize a basic equality of rights is unjust in his attitude toward minority groups.
> MINOR: Some of our fellow citizens *are* unwilling to recognize a basic equality of rights.
> CONCLUSION: So they are unjust in their attitude toward minority groups.

Given this as the basic argument, we can do all sorts of things to develop and expand it—either by way of explanation or defense of the premises or by way of a further development of the conclusion. The following paragraph is an example of how such an argument can be developed (analyze it as you read).

> One of the keystones of our American democracy is the recognition of a basic equality of rights. This doesn't mean, of course, that all men are equal in the sense that they are equally endowed with the same set of talents. As a matter of fact, all men are *different*. However, the fact is that all men *as* men are born with equal rights, such as the right to life, liberty, and the pursuit of happiness, and this fact is guaranteed in the very Constitution of the United States. Unfortunately, however, there are many people—in our own country— who still don't recognize a truth as self-evident as this; witness, for example, their attitude toward the Negro. These men, I say, are our

fellow citizens, and they are the people who are unwilling to recognize a basic equality of rights. If you want further proof of my statement, look at all the discriminatory practices that are still so much a built-in feature of our society: the refusal to grant open housing, the resistance to integrated schools, recreational facilities, and the like. The story of prejudice against the Negro is a long and sordid story, so I won't go into all the details. The point is that many of our fellow citizens even to this day are unjust in their attitude toward minority groups because they are unwilling to recognize a basic equality of rights. The hidden assumption of my argument is something I need not fear to bring out into the open: anyone who is unwilling to recognize a basic equality of rights is unjust in his attitude toward minority groups.

At this stage of the argument the person who develops it may wish to proceed even further. He may want, for example, to give statistical evidence in support of his minor premise, he may like to give further examples of definite types of persons who are prejudiced, and so on. Yet the basic framework of the argument is as we have given it above, and it should be easy enough for the reader to detect it.

EXERCISE 11.2

Complete the following assignments.

1. Save up your newspapers for a week or so and cut out the editorials and syndicated columns. Analyze some of these arguments in class and proceed to draw up several arguments of your own as if you yourself were an editor or a columnist.
2. Examine some of the letters to the editor either in your local newspaper or in one of the national magazines. Do you find that these letters are based on argumentation or are they simply expressions of personal prejudice, name calling, and the like? Produce specific examples.

OTHER MODES OF ARGUMENTATION: Reductio ad Absurdum

Before we conclude this chapter, we should mention that there are various types of arguments that are not reducible to a syllogism or that are of such a nature that it would be impractical to attempt such a reduction. Arguments of this sort, to mention only a few, are those involving an *appeal to belief or authority,* the *employment of statistics, circumstantial evidence,* and the *reductio ad absurdum.*

A throughgoing study of these types of arguments would take us beyond the scope of our text. Such a study would involve a painstaking analysis of the *conditions* under which arguments of this sort are valid. The effectiveness, for example, of the *argument from belief* would depend upon such factors as whether the proposition presented for belief does or does not contradict any other truths that are known for a certainty and the competence and trustworthiness of the witness. Further, any argument based on *statistics* would have to be evaluated in terms of what the statistics are intended to prove in the first place, whether they are complete or incomplete; if incomplete, whether the samplings given are typical, and the like. Here we need only mention that the use of statistics requires in some instances at least an introductory analysis of statistics as an independent branch of knowledge. In the absence of the proper safeguards one is tempted to agree at times with the maxim, "Figures don't lie, but often the people who use them do."

A word should be said, finally, about a type of argument known as *reductio ad absurdum*—literally, "reducing to a point of absurdity." This type of argument is closely related to certain aspects of the hypothetical syllogism as we shall discuss it in the chapter that follows. It consists in drawing out the consequences of your opponent's position to show that they are absurd, contrary to fact, unacceptable, and so on.[1] The technique of the *reductio* is to grant your opponent's position for the sake of argument and go on to show that it leads to consequences that, more often than not, no reasonable person could accept.

The ways and means of recognizing this type of argument are varied. For example, a person may say, "If Communism is as great a system as you say it is, then how do you explain the fact that Red China is plagued with so many imponderable economic problems?" Rightly or wrongly, the person who is here introducing a *reductio* type of argument is trying to draw out the consequences of his opponent's position.

Examples:
1. If professors are as smart as they think they are, they wouldn't be content with such low salaries.
2. You say that your new "no interest" down-payment plan will actually save me money. That isn't what my husband tells me when he writes out the checks at the end of the month.

There are many ways of reducing something to a point of absurdity, but whichever way we follow, we should be careful not to draw out of our

---

[1] In its strictest interpretation this argument involves a reduction to a *logically* unacceptable because *inconsistent* conclusion—not just one that is unhappy in some way. We have chosen, however, to give the *reductio* this broader interpretation as stated above in the text.

opponent's position consequences that do not actually follow from it. On the other hand, if the consequences we set forth are valid, then we have for all practical intents shown his original position to be unacceptable, false, unsatisfactory, invalid, or the like.

EXERCISE 11.3

A. Evaluate the following.

1. Statistics prove that women are much better drivers than men because there are fewer recorded cases of accidents for women than for men.
2. The problem with the argument from authority is that you can never be sure of whom to believe. The answer, then, to this problem is, "Don't believe *anyone* except yourself."
3. You say that your university is one of the greatest in the United States. If that were the case, then you wouldn't have as many dropouts as you do because a 70 percent rate of freshman dropouts indicates a low level of intelligence among your student body.

B. Complete the following assignments.

1. Give your own illustration of an argument based on a misuse of statistics.
2. Give one example of what you consider to be a *valid* use of the *reductio ad absurdum,* another of its *invalid* use.

chapter 12

Symbolic Logic

A Practical Approach

Traditional and Symbolic Logic
"Truth-Functional" Statements
The Conditional Syllogism
Underlying Theory
Disjunctive Propositions and Syllogisms
Conjunctive Propositions and Syllogisms
The Dilemma

The aim of this chapter is to acquaint the student with symbolic logic from a practical point of view. Toward this end the symbolism employed will not be rigorously defined. The practical value of translation and recognition of form will be emphasized. For a formally rigorous approach a separate chapter is provided (see pp. 188–216). In the present chapter we shall devote our attention to hypothetical, disjunctive, and conjunctive statements, together with the various types of arguments to which they give rise. In the last section of the chapter we shall treat the various forms of the dilemma.

TRADITIONAL AND SYMBOLIC LOGIC

The material of our previous chapters has been developed within the framework of a traditional logic which is both realistic and practical. Our approach has been realistic insofar as we have stressed the fundamental importance of the relationship between mind and reality; it has been practical to the extent that we have applied what we learned to the language of everyday discourse. The present chapter will be equally realistic and practical, but it will be developed with a more technical approach to the subject through the elementary use of certain symbolic forms. Further, while

the material of the last few chapters has focused on categorical argumentation and debate, we shall now encounter such basic forms as "if . . .
then," "either . . . or" arguments that are based, not on simple categorical statements, but on statements that are "truth-functional" in their meaning and implication. Take the following as examples:

1. If you light the fuse, then the dynamite will explode.
2. Either the senator has a private income or else he is dishonest.

If you examine these propositions carefully, you will note that they are
made up of at least two simple propositions, and depending on the relationship between their constitutive parts, they will, as compound statements,
(see Chapter 5) be either true or false. As we shall soon see in greater
detail, the truth value (whether the statement is true or false) of such
compound statements will depend on the truth value of their parts as well
as on the relationship that exists between them.

In general, one of the chief advantages of symbolic logic lies in the
fact that symbols greatly facilitate our thinking processes. In this sense an
important justification for the development of symbolic logic stems from
certain practical considerations, such as occur in the handling of long and
complicated arguments. Finally, symbolic logic, in contrast to the traditional
forms, is more readily applicable in the physical sciences. Physicists and
engineers, for example, use symbolic logic to determine the efficiency of
circuits and to simplify complicated ones. The logic of classes and relations
is also important in some areas of biology; from a theoretical point of view
it has helped to clarify many of the fundamental concepts of mathematics.

"TRUTH-FUNCTIONAL" STATEMENTS

Our study of syllogisms in this chapter will be based on the use of
three types of truth-functional statements:

1. the "if . . . then" type, known as the *conditional* or *hypothetical;*
2. the "either . . . or" type, known as the *disjunctive;* and
3 the "cannot be both" type, a kind of *conjunctive* statement.

Note: Modern logicians do not ordinarily single out the last type of
statement for the degree of prominence we shall give it in the latter
part of this chapter. Our purpose in treating it is based on the practical
value of the statement and the type of syllogism to which it gives rise.
If any confusion arises as to the meaning and use of this statement, we
shall refer to it as a type of "negative conjunctive."

Each of these types will be studied in its turn, but we want to make it clear at this point that each of them may be referred to as a "truth-functional" statement. These are simply statements whose truth or falsity depends either upon the truth or falsity of their parts or *on the relationship that exists between them.*

Conditional (If . . . Then) Statements

Few statements are of such fundamental importance in logic as conditionals, and every conditional consists of two parts, respectively known as the antecedent (the "if" clause) and the consequent (what follows from the "if"):

Antecedent	Consequent
If men love danger,	they will perish in it.
If a man works,	then he deserves his labor's reward.
If you are amused,	you will smile.

Most conditionals are such that the condition expressed in their antecedent is sufficient to guarantee the fulfillment of their consequent; lacking this requirement, a conditional proposition is considered to be *false.* Thus, if I assert that, *given* a case of measles (M), a person will be sick (S), and it turns out that someone with measles is not sick $(\sim S)$, then my proposition is false. If the consequent does *not* follow from the antecedent that is given, then the proposition *as a whole* is *false.*

A fuller understanding of conditional propositions should alert us to the many different ways in which they are expressed. Although the word "if" is the ordinary sign of a conditional, we also use such expressions as

provided that	in the event that
assuming that	in case of
supposing that	unless
on this hypothesis	

From the standpoint of symbolic logic, a conditional proposition is expressed by the form "if p, then q," and more frequently by the "horseshoe" symbol, "$p \supset q$"—according to which use p and q are taken respectively as the antecedent and consequent of the conditional statement. Here it is important to note as well that lower-case letters, such as p, q, and r, usually represent types of propositions. When logicians wish to represent the form of any proposition or argument, these are the letters they use. Capital letters are used to represent *particular* propositions. Thus the lower-case letters of the alphabet are called *variables.* They give us the *form* of a proposition. The following are examples of translations of particular propositions into symbolic notation:

Proposition	Abbreviated Symbol
If you study you will learn.	$S \supset L$
If you follow your conscience, you will be happy.	$C \supset H$
If you get lost, your mother will worry.	$L \supset W$

Some further observations should be brought to mind at this point, and among them the importance of placing a negative sign, $\sim$, in front of any part of a conditional statement that is negative. Thus, "If you do not eat, you will lose weight," should (because of the negative antecedent) be expressed in some such manner as follows: $\sim E \supset L$.

The word "unless" is frequently a source of difficulty in dealing with conditionals because of its negative import. A good procedure to follow is simply to translate the word "unless" into the expression "if not" as follows:

Unless you run, you will lose the race: $\sim R \supset L$

The use of symbols in all such instances is the surest method of laying bare the logical structure of our proposition.

EXERCISE 12.1

Draw up your own set of symbols for each of the following propositions. If you encounter the word "unless" translate it as "if not." Should some of the examples below invert the order of antecedent and consequent, reverse them according to their logical order. Thus: "The men will not fight unless they get something to eat" would be expressed $\sim E \supset \sim F$.

1. Unless you water this plant, it will die.
2. If Bill is right, then I'm a liar.
3. If the President is taking his nap, nobody can sign this bill.
4. You won't learn unless you study.
5. Joan will go if Mary does.

Conditionals and Their Equivalents

Before we examine the conditional (hypothetical) syllogism, a few further points should be brought to mind concerning conditional propositions. Of first importance is the method of denying conditionals. This is certainly not accomplished by contradicting one or the other of its parts, but rather by showing that the *consequent does not follow* from its antecedent. Accordingly, should someone say, "If you start reading this book you won't be able to put it down," you can deny the statement by saying that even if you start the book, it is quite possible for you to put it down (to stop reading it). Another way of denying propositions, the conditional included, is by the use of the expression, "It is not the case that. . . ." Thus, symbolically, $p \supset q$ is denied by a denial of the proposition as a whole: $\sim(p \supset q)$.

Further, in the case of the ordinary conditional it is important to know that the antecedent and consequent are not equivalent to each other. Thus because $p \supset q$ it does not follow that $q \supset p$.

So much at this stage for "ordinary" conditional statements. We must now give some attention to the identifying expression "If, and only if." The purpose of this expression is to show that the condition specified in the antecedent is not only the *sufficient* condition for the consequent to be true, but that it is a *necessary* condition as well.

> *Example:* If, and only if, men lay down their weapons, will they have peace.

This statement makes two affirmations: if men lay down their weapons, they will have peace; and *under no other condition* is it possible for them to have peace. The effect of such a statement is to assert the equivalence or the possibility of making a simple conversion between the antecedent and the consequent. Thus, in the case of the biconditional (*and in that case alone*) are the antecedent and consequent reversible ($p \supset q$ and $q \supset p$). Because of this equivalence, symbolic logicians use a triple bar as a means of representing this type of statement: $p \equiv q$.

Let us note the difference between an "ordinary" conditional and a biconditional. An ordinary conditional lays down a condition and states that if *this* condition is fulfilled, then does the consequent follow. The condition given is *sufficient* for the consequent. However, it is *not* necessary, in the sense that it is the *only* condition under which such a consequent may take place. Accordingly, "If you are a plumber, you need tools," states that your being a plumber is the *sufficient* condition for your needing tools, but not a necessary condition. Since you might be a carpenter or an appliance repairman and still need tools, in this case it is possible to have a variety of antecedents that lead to one and the same consequent ("needing tools"). Not so, however, for the biconditional: in its case the condition laid down is the only one possible to justify the consequent—which is equivalent to saying that it is an exclusive condition or that the antecedent and consequent are convertible to each other.

Note: If you make a comparison here between ordinary categoricals, such as *"S is P,"* and exclusive statements, "Only *S* is *P,"* you will find some similarity between an ordinary and a biconditional.

EXERCISE 12.2

A. See if you can reverse these statements and explain your results:

1. If you live in Arizona, you will find that the summers are hot.
2. If you are a man, then you have powers of sensation.
3. If the electricity is turned off, the lights will go out.

B. Tell whether you think the following biconditional is true or false. Discuss your answer.

If, and only if, a man is elected, he will become President of the United States.

THE CONDITIONAL SYLLOGISM

Hypothetical syllogisms are of various types, and one such type is known as the pure hypothetical.

Example:
If you are a politician, you are interested in securing votes.
If you are interested in securing votes, you must be attentive to the needs of the people

∴ If you are a politician, you must be attentive to the needs of the people.

The symbolic expression of the above type of argument is:

$$
\begin{array}{l}
p \supset q \\
q \supset r \\
\hline
\therefore p \supset r
\end{array}
$$

The procedure in constructing this type is to make the consequent of the original statement the antecedent of the one that follows and then to draw the conclusion as indicated. Another such type of argument is the hypothetical counterpart of the sorites already examined in Chapter 9.

Example:
If you love your fellow man, you will seek peace.
If you seek peace, you will wish to avoid war.
If you wish to avoid war, you will favor disarmament.
If you favor disarmament, you will cut down on the cost of arms.

If you love your fellow man, you will cut down on the cost of arms.

The symbolic expression of the argument is:

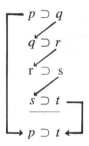

Of much greater importance than either of the above types is the hypothetical syllogism as we ordinarily understand it—one whose minor premise and conclusion either reaffirm ("posit") or deny ("sublate") the parts of the original statement. Basically there is a right way and a wrong way of setting up each mood of the conditional syllogism, namely, for the "positing" (*modus ponens*) and the "sublating" (*modus tollens*) mood.

1. *Positing Mood* (*modus ponens*)
    Right way
    MAJOR: If you love your neighbor, you will help him.
    MINOR: You do love him.
    CONCLUSION: You will help him.

    Wrong way
    MAJOR: If you love your neighbor, you will help him.
    MINOR: You are helping him.
    CONCLUSION: So you love him.

The symbolic expression of the above arguments is as follows:

Right Way	*Wrong Way*
$L \supset H$	$L \supset H$
L	H
$\therefore \quad H$	$\therefore L$

According to correct procedure in the positing mood (*modus ponens*), we accept the antecedent *in the minor premise* and the consequent in the conclusion. To do the reverse is to commit the *fallacy of positing the consequent.*

We have just shown the right way and the wrong way for setting up a conditional syllogism in the positing mood. Let us now do the same for the sublating mood (*modus tollens*):

1. *Sublating mood* (*modus tollens*)
   Right way
   MAJOR: If you eat spicy foods, you will get ulcers.
   MINOR: You do *not* have ulcers.
   CONCLUSION: So you are *not* eating spicy foods.

   Wrong way
   MAJOR: If you eat spicy foods, you will get ulcers.
   MINOR: You are *not* eating spicy foods.
   CONCLUSION: So you will *not* get ulcers.

The symbolic expression of the argument is as follows:

$$
\begin{array}{cc}
\textit{Right way} & \textit{Wrong way} \\
S \supset U & S \supset U \\
\sim U & \sim S \\
\hline
\therefore \sim S & \therefore \quad \sim U
\end{array}
$$

Here the *correct* procedure is to sublate (reject, deny, contradict, remove) the *consequent* in the minor premise and the antecedent in the conclusion.

Practical Observations

Much confusion can be avoided in this type of syllogism if we remember that it is always the minor premise that determines the "mood." Thus, if in the minor we "take over" one of the parts of the major premise, our syllogism is in the "positing" mood; if the minor *contradicts* one part of the major, we have a case of the "sublating" mood.

The rules, then, for the conditional syllogism are the essence of simplicity itself:

1. Positing Mood
   a. Minor posits antecedent
   b. Conclusion posits consequent

2. Sublating mood
   a. Minor sublates consequent
   b. Conclusion sublates antecedent

EXERCISE 12.3

Specify the mood of the following forms and tell whether they are valid or invalid; if invalid, name the fallacy.

1. $p \supset q, p, \therefore q$
2. $p \supset q, q, \therefore p$
3. $\sim p \supset q, q, \therefore \sim p$
4. $\sim p \supset q, \sim q, \therefore p$
5. $\sim p \supset \sim q, q, \therefore p$
6. $p \supset \sim q, p, \therefore \sim q$
7. $p \supset \sim q, \sim q \therefore p$
8. $p \supset q, \sim p, \therefore \sim q$
9. $\sim p \supset \sim q, \sim p, \therefore \sim q$
10. $\sim p \supset q, p, \therefore q$

UNDERLYING THEORY

We have just seen which procedure is valid for each of the moods of the mixed conditional syllogism. Let us briefly explain *why* these procedures must be followed.

Positing Mood

As previously noted, the ordinary conditional (in contrast to an "if and only if" type of statement) is such that any number of antecedents could lead to one and the same consequent. Thus:

If I oversleep,
If I read the morning newspaper,
If I miss the bus,
If I get involved in an accident,   *I shall be late for class.*
If I go to the wrong building,
Etc.

If we *posit* any one of the above antecedents, we are correct in positing also the consequent "I shall be late for class." Suppose, however, that *"I am late for class."* In that case we may not infer conversely the fulfillment of any one of the *specific* antecedents above, for the simple reason that the mere positing of the consequent leaves *indefinite* the question as to *which* of the antecedents has been fulfilled.

Given this sequence, it is right to posit one of the above antecedents in the minor and the consequent in the conclusion, *but not the other way around*. Only if the major premise were a biconditional would both procedures be correct.

Sublating Mood

We now ask the question: Why is it necessary to sublate the consequent in the minor and the antecedent in the conclusion? Note that we are correct in making the following inference:

> MAJOR: If I oversleep, I shall be late for class.
> MINOR: But I was *not* late for class.
> CONCLUSION: So I did *not* oversleep.

Here the *nonfulfillment* of the consequent justifies our inference of the nonfulfillment of any one or all of its possible antecedents. Since "I was not late for class," *none* of the conditions that might have induced me to be late were fulfilled.

> I did not oversleep.
> I did not read the newspaper.
> I did not miss the bus.
> I did not get involved in an accident.
> I did not go to the wrong building.

Conversely, it would be wrong to proceed from the rejection of a *specific* antecedent to the rejection of the consequent thus:

> If I oversleep, I shall be late for class.
> I did *not* oversleep.
> I was *not* late for class.

According to our example, I could still be late for class even though I did not oversleep—since the consequent could have eventuated for some *other* reason, such as missing the bus. The correct procedure, then, for the sublating mood is to remove the consequent in the minor and the antecedent in the conclusion.

EXERCISE 12.4

A. Complete the following both in the positing and sublating moods:

1. If A is M, then A is also N.
2. If non-A is B, then X is Y.
3. If every X is a Y, then no non-X is a Z.
4. If none of the D's are E's, then all of the E's are F's.
5. If some of the non-P's are Q's, then all of of the non-Q's are R's.

B. Determine by symbols as given whether the following examples are valid or invalid; name the mood and the fallacy if there is a fallacy. Keep in mind that a biconditional may be valid either way (that is, regardless of the procedures outlined above):

1. If our jeep is in working order, we shall go to the mountains. But we are not going to the mountains. Ergo (meaning "therefore"). (Use J and M)
2. If you drink this water you will quench your thirst. Since you did not drink, you are still thirsty. (Use W and T)
3. If the plane runs out of fuel, we shall have to make an emergency landing. Since there is no need for an emergency landing, the plane did not run out of fuel. (Use P and E)
4. If you do not practice the piano, you will not play in the concert. Since you are practicing, it follows that you will play. (Use $\sim P$ and $\sim C$)
5. If this lion is hungry, he will eat human flesh. Since he is not hungry, he will not eat me. (Use L and E)
6. If Jack does nothing but work, he will grow dull. Jack has grown dull. Ergo. (Use J and D)
7. If it rains, I shall not have to sprinkle. Fortunately, it is raining. Ergo. (Use R and $\sim S$)
8. If, and only if, you are elected will you become President of the United States. But you have not been elected. Ergo. (Use E and P)

DISJUNCTIVE PROPOSITIONS AND SYLLOGISMS

So far we have been talking about conditional statements, the component parts of which are known as antecedent and consequent. Now we shall begin speaking of disjunctives, whose parts are known as "alternatives."

A disjunctive proposition is an "either . . . or" type of statement which may be taken either strictly or loosely. A strict disjunctive means one *or* the other to the exclusion of the other, in the sense that if one alternative is true, the other must be false and vice versa.

Example: The will is either free or not free.

Such a statement cannot be true unless one of its parts is true *and* the other false. In a case where both parts are true or where both parts are false, the statement itself is false. According to the meaning of this statement, the alternatives are such that the "either" of one alternative is taken *to the exclusion* of the other.

Normally a disjunctive statement is taken in a much looser sense—in the sense that both parts *may* be true, but it is *impossible for both of them to be false*. If I say that your sleepiness was caused either by a drug or from sheer exhaustion, it is possible that *both* alternatives are true. The truth of such a statement, then, depends only on one factor, that *at least one part must be true*. Accordingly, the only condition under which such a statement would be false would be when both of its parts are false. Symbolically, the *loose* disjunctive may be expressed by means of a wedge, as follows: $p \vee q$.

For purposes of reasoning, the disjunctive syllogism is of crucial importance, especially in the logic of induction. For now, however, we must see under which conditions disjunctive reasoning is valid. Unless it is clearly indicated to the contrary, we shall assume that disjunctive syllogisms have a loose disjunctive like the following as their major premise:

> Bill came home late either because he ate out or because he went to a movie.

The sense of this statement is such that it is possible for both of the alternatives to be true, though it would be wrong to suppose that both of them are false. This being so, the question arises whether we can set up a syllogism in the *positing* mood.

Example:
MAJOR: Bill came home late either because he ate out or because he went to a movie.
MINOR: Bill ate out.
CONCLUSION: So he did *not* go to a movie.

In this example we posited one alternative in the minor and sublated the other in the conclusion. To do this was to assume in effect that if one alternative is true, the other is false, and this we may *not* do in the case of a loose disjunctive. In other words, syllogisms that have a loose disjunctive as their major premise are *invalid* in the *positing* mood.[1] Thus if we use symbols for our example above we can see that either method of "positing" as below is invalid:

	Wrong	
MAJOR:	$A \vee M$	$A \vee M$
MINOR:	A	M
CONCLUSION:	$\sim M$	$\sim A$

Since the method of positing (in the minor premise) does not work for this type of syllogism, let us reverse the procedure by sublating in the minor and positing in the conclusion.

Example:
MAJOR: Bill came home late either because he ate out or because he went to a movie.
MINOR: Bill did *not* eat out.
CONCLUSION: So he went to a movie.

Assuming the original statement to be true, our reasoning is perfectly correct because we can now assume from the falsity of one alternative (see the minor premise) that the other must be true (see the conclusion). If we use symbols for the syllogism, we find that either of the methods below are valid:

	Right	
MAJOR:	$A \vee M$	$A \vee M$
MINOR:	$\sim A$	$\sim M$
CONCLUSION:	M	A

On the basis of the procedure outlined, we may accordingly formulate the following rules:

1. Unless otherwise specified (that is, as strict disjunctive), disjunctive syllogisms are invalid in the positing mood.

---

[1] Whether any disjunctive syllogism is valid in the *positing* mood is dependent in each case on the strictly disjunctive character of its major premise. *Only if the major premise is strictly and properly disjunctive is it permissible to employ a disjunctive syllogism in the positing mood.* Except in the case of formal contradictories, the possibility of doing this is clearly dependent on the *matter* of the proposition expressed since the copula "either . . . or" leaves it open to question whether any given proposition is strictly disjunctive or not.

2. To construct a disjunctive syllogism in the sublating mood, remove or contradict one or more of the parts in the minor, and posit (accept) the remaining one in the conclusion.

Note: Disjunctive premises need not be restricted to two and only two parts. Especially when the parts are multiple and when one or more of them are negative in form, one should get in the habit of marking off the parts by number, as "1," "2," "3," and of using such symbols as A or $\sim A$, B or $\sim B$, C or $\sim C$.

Example: Your sickness was caused by overwork, by too little sleep, or by an improper diet.

Represent this proposition as follows:

$$\begin{array}{ccc} 1 & 2 & 3 \\ O & v\ S\ v & I \end{array}$$

In the minor premise sublate or contradict two of the parts (using a dot ($\cdot$) to signify "and"):

$$\begin{array}{cc} 1 & 2 \\ \sim O\ \cdot & \sim S \end{array}$$

In the conclusion posit the remaining part:

$$\begin{array}{c} 3 \\ I \end{array}$$

EXERCISE 12.5

A. Tell whether the following forms are valid or not.

1. $p \lor q, \sim p, \therefore q$
2. $\sim p \lor q, \sim p, \therefore \sim q$
3. $p \lor \sim q, q, \therefore p$
4. $\sim p \lor \sim q, \sim p, \therefore q$
5. $\sim p \lor \sim q, p, \therefore \sim q$

B. Tell whether the following syllogisms are valid or not.

1. Either Mike went to the store or he went downtown. Since he went downtown, he didn't go to the store. (Use S and D)

2. Either we play ball or we eat hot dogs. Since we did not eat hot dogs, we played ball. (Use *B* or *E*)
3. The ladder slipped either because I was too heavy for it or because it was made of too light a wood. Obviously I was too heavy for it, so it was not made of too light a wood. (Use *H* and *W*)
4. The car ran out of gas or the transmission broke down or it ran into a brick wall. But the transmission did not break down, nor did the car run into a brick wall. So it ran out of gas. (Use *R, B,* and *W*)
5. Either Jim doesn't know how to read or he doesn't know how to spell. But, as a matter of fact, he does know how to read, so it follows that he doesn't know how to spell. (Use ~*R* and ~*S*)

CONJUNCTIVE PROPOSITIONS AND SYLLOGISMS

We have already seen what is meant by a conjunctive statement in logic.

Example: Bill is going to the movie and Mary is going to the ball.

Symbolically, this type of statement is represented as follows (the dot standing for the word "and"): *B* · *M*. As we have seen, the truth of this type of statement is dependent upon both (or all) of its parts being true. Some teachers include the following as a syllogism:

$$B \cdot M$$
$$\underline{B}$$
$$M$$

Of much more importance, however, is the conjunctive statement which states the impossibility of two or more parts being simultaneously true:

You cannot eat cookies and talk at the same time.

In modern logic this type of statement is usually rendered in the general form "~$(p \cdot q)$" or, in the case of our example, "~$(E \cdot T)$." Such a statement is negative in form and may be taken as the contradictory of the conjunctive in the ordinary sense. The meaning of the statement may best be seen by contrast with a loose disjunctive:

Loose disjunctive: at least one part must be *true;* it is impossible for both to be *false.*
Negative conjunctive: at least one part must be *false;* it is impossible for both to be *true.*

Let us proceed, then, to a (negative) conjunctive syllogism—one whose major premise is the sort of proposition we have just examined. To be *valid,* such a syllogism must *posit* one of the alternatives in the minor and *sublate* the remainder in the conclusion. To do this is to say in effect that because one part is true the other must be false.

Example:

MAJOR: You cannot be a good businessman and be indifferent to money.
MINOR: Murray Windfall *is* a good businessman.
CONCLUSION: He is not indifferent to money.

Symbolically:

$$\sim (G \cdot I)$$
$$\underline{\quad G \quad}$$
$$\therefore \quad \sim I$$

The syllogism is valid because it is constructed in the positing mood.

However, it is *invalid* to place this type of syllogism in the *sublating mood.*

Example:

MAJOR: You cannot be both an American and a European.
MINOR: You are *not* a European.
CONCLUSION: You are an American.

As a matter of fact, you may be an Asiatic. The above syllogism is invalid for the simple reason that the nontruth of one alternative does not necessarily imply the truth of the other. Both alternatives of the major premise might conceivably be false.

To sum up, the (negative) conjunctive syllogism is valid only in the *positing* mood.

As a practical means of handling this type of syllogism, it is important to separate the negative prefix ("You cannot," "It is impossible," and so on) from the alternatives listed and then to number the alternatives.[2]

Example:

1   2

MAJOR: One cannot *eat his cake* and *have it too.*

1

MINOR: Jasper is eating his cake.

2

CONCLUSION: He *no longer "has"* it.

---

[2] In other words, the "not" of the word "cannot" does not make the alternatives negative. For this reason, you must size up the alternatives independently.

Better yet, symbolize your argument as follows:

$$\sim(E \cdot H)$$
$$\underline{\hspace{1.5cm} E \hspace{1.5cm}}$$
$$\therefore \quad \sim H$$

EXERCISE 12.6

A. Tell whether the following forms are valid or not.

1. $\sim(p \cdot q), \sim p, \therefore q$
2. $\sim(\sim p \cdot q), \sim p, \therefore \sim q$
3. $\sim(\sim p \cdot q), \sim q, \therefore p$
4. $\sim(p \cdot q), q, \therefore \sim p$
5. $\sim(\sim p \cdot \sim q), p, \therefore \sim q$

B. Specify the mood of the following examples and determine whether they are valid or not.

1. You can't be a good politician and despise public opinion. But some professors do not despise public opinion, so they are good politicians. (Use G and O)
2. It's impossible to read and sleep simultaneously. Since you are reading, you can't be sleeping. (Use R and S)
3. It is not the case that a man can both love history and ignore the past. But I don't care for history. (Use H and P)
4. You cannot go on indefinitely ignoring your health and expect to live to a ripe old age. But you do expect to live to a ripe old age. (Use I and A)
5. A potato can't be both hot and cold. This potato is not hot. (Use H and C)

THE DILEMMA

The dilemma is a hybrid type of syllogism which combines the use of both conditional and disjunctive propositions. It is a type of argument that, if well constructed, can prove highly effective; yet, as we shall see, it is one that is also subject to serious abuse.

Since a dilemma in the sublating mood is of very infrequent occurrence, we shall restrict our attention here to the two most common varieties, both of which are in the positing mood.

Simple Constructive Dilemma

Every dilemma has as its major premise *two* conditional propositions. The major premise of a simple constructive dilemma is one having *two different antecedents,* both leading to the *same consequent.*

Example:
MAJOR: If this thief attempts a getaway, *he will be caught.* If he remains at the scene of his crime, *he will be caught.*

The *minor* premise of this type of dilemma *disjunctively posits* the two antecedents of the major. Thus:

MINOR: This thief will either attempt a getaway or he will remain at the scene of his crime.

The conclusion *categorically posits* the single consequent of the major:

CONCLUSION: He will be caught.

Here it is worth noting that the major premise of this type of dilemma is frequently expressed in the form of a single statement.

Whether this thief attempts a getaway or whether he remains at the scene of the crime, he will be caught.

A glance at this example shows that the dilemma follows the same pattern as the rules for the conditional syllogism, already given in this chapter:

Minor posits antecedents.
Conclusion posits consequent.

Symbolically, a simple dilemma may be expressed thus:

$$(p \supset q) \cdot (r \supset q) \ [(\text{or}) \ (p \cdot r) \supset q]$$
$$\underline{p \vee r}$$
$$\therefore q$$

Complex Constructive Dilemma

The complex constructive dilemma differs from the one above in that the two antecedents of the major premise lead to *two* different consequents:

Example.

> MAJOR: If a politician votes according to his conscience, he will lose the support of his constituents. If he votes according to the desires of his constituents, he violates his conscience.

Here *the minor disjunctively posits the antecedents of the major:*

> MINOR: This politician will vote either according to his conscience or according to the desires of his constituents.

Since the major premise has two different consequents, it is necessary to posit both of them *disjunctively* in the conclusion:

> CONCLUSION: He will either lose the support of his constituents or violate his conscience.

Symbolically a complex dilemma appears thus:

$$(p \supset q) \cdot (r \supset s)$$
$$\underline{p \lor r}$$
$$\therefore q \lor s$$

It would be a formal violation of the rules of the constructive dilemma to posit the consequent(s) in the minor and the antecedents in the conclusion (*fallacy of positing the consequent*).

In criticizing a dilemma on *material* grounds, it is necessary to examine carefully the *truth* of the major and minor premises.

Major Premise

Since the major is *conditional* in form, you deny its truth by pointing out that an alleged consequent does not follow from its given antecedent. To do this is to "take the dilemma by the horns."

Minor Premise

Deny the minor premise, which should be a *strict disjunctive,* by showing that the alternatives given are either incomplete or not mutually exclusive. This procedure is more commonly known as "escaping between the horns of a dilemma."

A Famous Dilemma

Protagoras the Sophist agreed to teach Eualthus the art of pleading, on the condition that Eualthus pay him one half of the fee upon completion of his course and the other half after he [Eualthus] had won his first case in court. Because of Eualthus' failure, upon completion of the course, to practice law, Protagoras decided to collect the other half of the fee. To do this he initiated a court action against Eualthus. As the case came to court Eualthus decided to conduct his own defense. The substance of Protagoras' appeal was as follows:

> If I win this case, Eualthus must pay *by order of the court;* if I lose, he must pay me *by the terms of our contract.* I shall either win the case or lose it. In either event Eualthus must pay the fee.

The following was Eualthus' rebuttal:

> If I win this case, I shall *not* have to pay by reason of the court's decision. If I lose this case, I shall *not* have to pay by reason of the terms of the contract. I shall either win or lose. In either event I shall not have to pay.

Since the appeal of both these men was directed to the court, neither of them was consistent in his appeal to the terms of the contract (that is, *against* the order of the court). Accordingly, if Protagoras lost the case, he had no right (against the decision of the court) to collect his fee—that is, by the original terms of the contract. He, of course, might have initiated another court action, but under the circumstances that was beside the point. Equally, if Eualthus lost, the decision of the court again would have been binding *against* the terms of the contract. Neither Protagoras nor Eualthus could "have it both ways."

EXERCISE 12.7

Invent symbols for the following dilemmas and decide whether they are simple or complex. Evaluate each for the truth value of its premises.

1. If you live only for money, you will be unhappy, and if you despise money, you will be unhappy. Either you live only for money or you despise it. Either way you will be unhappy.

2. If I get too much sleep, it interferes with my work because it makes me feel dull; I also feel dull if I get too little sleep—in which case I

still have difficulty with my work. Either way I have problems. (Reformulate this example as you find best.)

3. If I go to the circus, I neglect my math; if I stay home and study, I shall miss a lot of fun. Either I go to the circus or stay home and miss out on the fun.

A good deal of our everyday reasoning is hypothetical; that is, it is reasoning of the sort that involves the use of conditions and alternatives as a practical means of resolving doubts. Thus a golfer may reason:

> Either my drive landed in the woods somewhere near that set of trees or it got lost in the weeds. But as best I can tell, it traveled about fifty feet beyond this patch of weeds, so I'll look for it near one of these trees.

This example is a typical illustration of the role that hypothetical inference plays in the *problem-solving techniques* that we employ in our everyday lives. Indeed, the success of these techniques is very largely dependent on our ability to "size up" likely alternatives (as inductive hypotheses) which *in relation to a given set of circumstances* are complete and mutually exclusive. Their periodic failure, on the other hand, is most often characterized by the omission of some alternative which, though obvious enough in itself, for one reason or another is overlooked. It is thus that the dramatic success of many a mystery story hinges on the reader's failure to take into account some one alternative (hypothesis) that he should have been considering "all along."

Chart 12.1 (p. 168) is a summary of the different types of syllogisms presented in this chapter.

EXERCISE 12.8

The following exercise contains a variety of the types of arguments we have been studying in this chapter. Read the argument as a whole before determining the type of argument, its mood, whether it is valid. Write out in your notebook the leading premises together with the conclusion.

1. *Harassed Mother:* If I pick up Janie at school today, I'll miss my appointment with the dentist because the dental appointment is set up for 3:00 P.M. Yet if I do keep my dental appointment, I'll end up spending more than our monthly budget allows—because the money I would give to the dentist has already been spent to buy Jimmy a new pair of shoes. Well, either I pick up Janie at school or I keep the

Chart 12.1 Syllogisms

Type		Structure	Positing Mood		Sublating Mood	
Conditional	MAJOR:	Conditional				
	MINOR:	Categorical	Posits antecedent		Sublates consequent	
	CONCLUSION:	Categorical	Posits consequent		Sublates antecedent	
			Strict	**Loose**	**Strict**	**Loose**
Disjunctive	MAJOR:	Disjunctive				
	MINOR:	Categorical	Posits one alternative	*Invalid*	Sublates alternative(s)	Same as for strict
	CONCLUSION:	Categorical	Sublates remaining alternative(s)	*Invalid*	Posits remaining alternative	Same as for strict
Negative Conjunctive	MAJOR:	Conjunctive				
	MINOR:	Categorical	Posits one alternative		*Invalid*	
	CONCLUSION:	Categorical	Sublates the other alternative			
			Simple	**Complex**	**Simple ***	**Complex ***
Dilemma	MAJOR:	Two conditionals	Different antecedents Same consequent	Same antecedent Different consequents	Different antecedents Different consequents	Different antecedents Different consequents
	MINOR:	Disjunctive	Disjunctively posits antecedents	Disjunctively posits antecedents	Disjunctively sublates consequents	Disjunctively sublates consequents
	CONCLUSION:	Disjunctive (or categorical)	Categorically posits consequent	Disjunctively posits consequents	Categorically sublates antecedent	Disjunctively sublates antecedents

* Rare

dental appointment, so either _____ or _____
_____. (Blanks are here used to indicate alternatives of the conclusion).

2. No one can pay his bills unless he has some source of income these days. Well, it so happens that the country can't be as bad off as a lot of people claim it to be because, as a matter of fact, most people *do* pay their bills. Optimistically, then, I would conclude that most people do have a source of income.

3. I can't understand why this horse never wants to move. So either you "get tough" with him and try using a whip, or you treat him as gently as a doll. If you get tough, he will just stand there as stubborn as a mule. If you're gentle, he won't move either because he'll stand there and just let you pet him all day. Either way the horse just refuses to move. (Incidentally, I think I'll sell him at an auction.)

4. You can't just keep slighting a girl, ditching her for dates, and everything like that and expect her to end up marrying you. As your father, Bill, I can speak from experience, since your mother was no different from the way girls are today. Well, anyway, you tell me you're in love with Mamie, but I find that pretty hard to believe because, as the saying goes, you "treat her like dirt." So take my advice when I say you shouldn't expect her to marry you at all.

5. My car always seems to be breaking down, and when it does, I could never figure out why. Well, things have changed to the point that now I know because I've taken a course in evening school on "How to Fix Your Own Car." (It's a lot more useful, by the way, than that insufferable course I had to take in logic.) So when my car breaks down, I figure it's either the motor that's wrong or the transmission or the brakes. Well, the motor on my car is okay, and so's the transmission. So any fool can figure out it's the brakes. Boy, I could never have figured that one out in logic, and as far as I'm concerned, no more liberal arts courses for me.

chapter 13

Selected Readings
The Logic of Inquiry

The Need for Induction
Observation
Mill's Methods
How to Construct Hypotheses
Fallacies of Induction
The Argument from Analogy
Summary

"The object of reasoning is to find out, from the consideration of what we already know, something else which we do not know. Consequently, reasoning is good if it be such as to give a true conclusion from true premises, and not otherwise. . . . We are doubtless, in the main, logical animals, but not perfectly so." [1]

To undertake an exhaustive analysis of induction would carry us beyond the scope of this text; we shall confine ourselves instead to its most basic aspects and to some of its practical uses.

THE NEED FOR INDUCTION

As a method of reasoning deduction is simple and direct, for given the truth of the premises and the validity of our reasoning process, we *know* the conclusion to be true. Not so with induction, which in the main operates on the level of what is *probably* true. Further, there is no set of rules for induction, nor is it reducible to formal reasoning, since the methods of induction are employed on a tentative, trial-and-error basis and are therefore constantly subject to revision and control.

---

[1] Charles Sanders Peirce, "The Fixation of Belief" in Max Fisch, ed., *Classical American Philosophers,* New York: Appleton-Century-Crofts, 1951, p. 57.

Suppose your car stops in the middle of the desert. Good as it may be to take stock of the situation at hand, no amount of reflection will *by itself* enable you to solve your problem. You must find out—by the use of logic or by any other means—what is wrong with your motor, and the only way of doing so is to begin by lifting up the hood of your car. Perhaps it is a case of a misplaced wire, or something else has gone amiss. If you are not a mechanic, or even if you are one but lacking the necessary tools and parts, the first thing you must do is to get word to the nearest garage. All these steps may be only the beginning of the solution to your problem, but they represent *some* kind of start. As for the rules, it is best to keep a cool head and try to resolve your problem one step at a time.

Induction, then, is different from deduction in that the problems of induction cannot be solved by insight and understanding alone but only by the right combination of what detectives call headwork and footwork. The footwork lies in seeking out persons from whom information can be had, in testing and checking hypotheses, clues, leads, and so on, and in corroborating one's results. The headwork depends on many factors, not the least of which is your power of judgment to evaluate data and to determine whether your hypotheses have any weight. In short, induction is no simple method of reasoning, since it normally involves the use of complicated procedures and techniques, especially in scientific problems. The present chapter does not intend to construct an elaborate theory of induction, but simply to acquaint the reader with certain basic methods and the ways of putting them to use.

In general, then, the *need* for induction—and hence also its importance—is evidenced not only by the peculiar nature of the problems of the positive sciences, but also by the nature of most problems that confront us in our everyday life, such as,

> why some of the more intelligent students in the class are receiving below average marks in their examinations;
> why the house, after having been painted only a year ago, needs to be painted again;
> why business production has fallen off in the last three months;
> how to locate a missing article.

What we want to learn is the unknown cause (or combination of causes) that adequately accounts for the "phenomenon" at hand. The very first step toward the solution of any problem of this kind is a *precise determination of the problem itself*. This, we say, is the first step in induction, a step that *directly* calls for the use, not of inference, but of careful, painstaking *observation*. It is a step that involves the gathering of all sorts of data relevant to the cause of the phenomenon we are seeking to explain.

OBSERVATION

The observational stage of induction is one of the most important from beginning to end, and by observation we do not mean simply "waiting for the results to come in." True enough, in the case of natural phenomena it is not we who arrange the experiment, but in a sense nature itself, as in the case of an eclipse of the sun or the moon. Yet even in situations like these we cannot be completely passive, since we need to devise such objects as filtered lenses to help our observations. For purposes of induction, then, observation usually requires an attitude of attention, of active listening and arranging on the part of the observer. Further, it involves a specific focus on the data, so as to lead, not merely to a general knowledge of the problem or situation at hand, but to a kind of understanding that will make us familiar with its most intimate details. Accordingly, it is not enough for an optometrist to know *in general* that a person needs glasses; he wants to know precisely and in mathematical terms which type of correction to prescribe, and to this end his observations must be accurate, orderly, and specific.

By way of further example, suppose that your car is using more gas than you think it should. The problem thus perceived is too general to allow a solution. With a view toward knowing exactly what the problem is, therefore, you begin actively to seek out answers to particular questions. Exactly how much gas have I been using per mile? Is the amount significantly more than it was a week, a month, or even a year ago? Have I changed my brand of gas? Am I doing more city driving than before? Am I using "regular" or "super" gas? When did I have my last motor tune-up? Such questions as these are, of course, related to the hypothesis stage of induction, but they cannot be completely separated from the observational stage, so that in practice the two stages dovetail. Generally speaking, to the extent that we are diligent in making careful and painstaking observations, to that extent is it easier to delineate the problem and arrive at a satisfactory solution.

Half the battle, then, toward the solution of an inductive problem is in the accurate assessment of the problem itself—witness, for example, the advantage of accurate and reliable testimony in the solution of a criminal case. On the other hand, pity the poor detective who gets no more than a garbled, emotional account from his potential witnesses. Yet given some degree of cooperation from those who are in a position to help, much wasted time and frustration can be avoided by making a good start, and no better start can be made than through observations that are painstaking, accurate, and complete.

EXERCISE 13.1

The purpose of the following exercise is to help you—consciously—to form the habit of pursuing relevant details.

1. Two men—one young, the other middle-aged—after an all-day hike in the mountains fail to show up at the place where their car is parked. When the car is still locked at midnight, the harassed father of the young man calls the county sheriff. To evaluate the situation, the sheriff asks the father the following questions. Of the questions asked, which ones do you think are (a) relevant, (b) of doubtful relevance, and (c) beside the point. In each case discuss your answer when discussion is needed, and at the end of the process add a few questions of your own.

    a. Exactly when did the two men start out on the hike?
    b. Which trail did they start out on?
    c. Did one or both of them take along a camera?
    d. How well supplied were they with water? With food? Did they bring any beer?
    e. Did they have ropes?
    f. Had they traveled the area before? When?
    g. What kind of footgear did they have—hiking boots, tennis shoes, some other kind?
    h. How old is the middle-aged man? (Other questions here?)
    i. Is he married and does he have children?
    j. Is the younger man enrolled at the local college?
    k. Does one or both of them know how to read?
    l. Did either of them bring a compass?
    m. Did they bring along a snakebite kit? A pair of dice?
    n. How many flashlights did they take?
    o. How old is the young man's mother?
    p. Did either or both of them bring a sleeping bag?
    q. Do you know whether either has suicidal tendencies?
    r. Does the middle-aged man have arthritis?
    s. Does either of them have a fear of high places?

2. Relative to the problem of lending the father of a family $10,000 for a mortgage on a home, prepare a form that he is expected to fill out. Indicate at the end of the form which questions you might consider irrelevent, of doubtful relevance, of greater importance.

3. Give your own examples of the need for careful observation.

MILL'S METHODS

An effective way of determining the relevant causes of a particular phenomenon is by the employment of *Mill's Methods*. Though not the last word on induction, these can be useful in helping us to understand the nature of inductive inference. They were elaborated by John Stuart Mill (1806–1873), the influential British philosopher and political scientist, whose work in logic, among other things, has remained valid in large part to this day. Of the five canons of induction he formulated, four are utilized in this section.

One of Mill's Methods is called the *Method of Agreement*. According to this method, it is permissible to infer that any factor ("cause") which appears in each context in which a particular phenomenon ("effect") appears is the cause of that phenomenon. Suppose that on a certain day four office workers develop stomach cramps right after lunch. Upon reflection, they remember that they have had the following for lunch:

> *First Worker:* The day's special, coffee, bread, and mineral water.
> *Second Worker:* A ham sandwich, coffee, bread, and mineral water.
> *Third Worker:* A fruit salad, milk, bread, and mineral water.
> *Fourth Worker:* A hamburger, soup, crackers, and mineral water.

From the list we are permitted to infer that the mineral water caused the stomach cramps. Of course, the cause of the cramps may be a combination of factors, but we can increase the probability of the mineral water's being the cause by gathering additional evidence or facts. For example, the probability could be increased by noting that in another office all those who had mineral water that day also developed cramps.

Another useful method for detecting causal relationships is called the *Method of Difference*. Suppose that a certain factor is *present* in a *particular* context in which a phenomenon is present but is *absent* in *all other* contexts in which the phenomenon in question is absent. In such a case we are permitted to infer that the absent factor is causally connected with the phenomenon in question. Suppose, again, that stomach cramps are developed among a group of office workers right after lunch. This time the following are given as the lunch menus:

> *First Worker:* A hamburger, bread, onion soup, and coffee. Developed cramps.
> *Second Worker:* The day's special, bread, coffee, but no onion soup. No cramps.

Third Worker: A hamburger, no bread, no onion soup, but had coffee. No cramps.

Fourth Worker: A hamburger, bread, no onion soup, and no coffee. No cramps.

Checking the above example, we see that the one case of stomach cramps ate onion soup as part of the meal. In all cases where no onion soup was eaten, no cramps developed. These considerations permit us to infer that the onion soup was the cause of the stomach cramps. Again this hypothesis may be either reinforced or discarded by checking with other people who ate in the same cafeteria.

What is known as the *Joint Method of Agreement and Difference* is simply a combination of the above two methods. From the fact that a certain factor is present when a particular phenomenon is present, and absent when the phenomenon is also absent, we can infer a causal relationship.

Another interesting method is that of *Concomitant Variation.* According to this, we can infer that, given a particular context, any factor which is present proportionately as a specific phenomenon is present, or inversely, is causally connected with the phenomenon in question. Suppose that in terms of the above example, the following data is presented:

First Worker: Drank half a glass of mineral water and had mild cramps.

Second Worker: Drank a full glass and had severe pains.

Third Worker: Drank two glasses and developed severe pains and nausca.

Fourth Worker: Drank three glasses, vomited, and had to be hospitalized.

From the above data we may infer a direct proportion between the amount of mineral water drunk and the severity of the ensuing sickness. We thus infer a causal relationship between the two.

EXERCISE 13.2

After examining each set of the following data with their respective conclusions, critically comment in the light of Mill's Methods:

1. A lawyer with a perfect record finally loses a case. He remembers that on the morning of the loss, he had drunk a glass of tomato juice. This was the first glass of tomato juice he had ever taken in his life. He concludes that the tomato juice affected his mental capacities and thus caused him to lose the case.

2. In 1742 the ship *Britannica* sailed for Australia. During the trip four members of the crew developed scurvy. During the trip, the diet of the scurvy cases consisted invariably of the following:

> *Breakfast:* Salted ham, bread, and water.
> *Lunch:* Salted ham, bread, and ale.
> *Dinner:* Salted ham, bread, and wine.

The rest of the crew's diet consisted invariably of the following:

> *Breakfast:* Salted ham, bread, and water.
> *Lunch:* Salted ham, bread, one lime, and water.
> *Dinner:* Salted ham, bread, and water.

Upon arrival, the captain concluded that the ale caused the scurvy.
3. One day a Chinese merchant's house caught fire. After the house was reduced to ashes, a very saporific odor filled his nostrils. Upon closer inspection he noticed that a pig had been caught in the house during the fire and had burned to death. He tasted part of the meat and, to his amazement, found it most delicious. He concluded that this delicacy could only be produced by burning down a house with a pig in it, and thereafter he went around advising his neighbors to burn down their houses in order to taste this unusual delicacy.
4. A man whose dog is very ill believes that salt is the cause of the illness. For the next three weeks he serves his dog nothing but the finest steak, leg of lamb, pork chops, and tender chicken, but all without salt. To his amazement and contentment, the dog recovers. He concludes that salt was the cause of the dog's illness.
5. After each night of heavy drinking a man wakes up with a splitting headache. One day he decides to examine all the things he had to drink during the previous four days. He makes out the following list:

> *Monday:* Vodka and orange juice, gin and orange juice, straight scotch.
> *Tuesday:* Straight gin, vodka and orange juice, rum and orange juice.
> *Wednesday:* Bourbon and orange juice, straight whiskey, and coffee.
> *Thursday:* Orange juice and tequila, orange juice and rum, orange juice and wine, orange juice and scotch, and orange juice plain.

He concludes that orange juice is the cause of his splitting headache on each consecutive morning of the night he drinks. To support his hypothesis, he recalls that his headache was most intense on the morning following his last day of drinking as recorded in the chart. Feeling sure of his discovery, he goes to the nearest bar with a happy smile on his face.

HOW TO CONSTRUCT HYPOTHESES

The construction of hypotheses is a central feature of all inductive inquiry, and a hypothesis is simply a tentative proposal for the solution of the problem at hand. The "framing of hypotheses," or the setting up of alternative methods of solution, is not a simple matter of logical technique; it involves familiarity with the details of the case at hand. Induction requires imagination, creativity, intuition, and pluck in addition to reflection.

In one of his essays, entitled "The Supremacy of Method," John Dewey sets forth an interesting definition of thinking as "deferred action" or "response to the doubtful as such." What Dewey has in mind is the importance—for purposes of induction—of deferring a determinate means of solution before we have given ourselves a chance to consider the real alternatives *reflectively*. There is no more serious temptation than that of impetuously "latching onto" the first hypothesis that comes to mind. Suppose that a student is getting poor grades. The immediate temptation of the parents is to blame the student for, let us say, being lazy. The parents leave out of account such possibilities as money worries, distractions of all sort (for which the student may not be to blame at all), health problems, or feelings of social insecurity. Their failure in such a situation is that of "hasty induction"—the fallacy of leaping to the first hypothesis that comes to mind without a careful examination of the evidence at hand. To think inductively, then, means in the language of Dewey to "defer action" until we have had a chance to reflect. No more important guideline can be offered than the following:

> *Withhold judgment until you have had a chance*
> *to examine the evidence at hand.*

The amount of essential evidence is another matter: some persons are too quick to judge without evidence and others too slow even when the time for judging is ripe. Unfortunately there is no one set method to determine the point of sufficiency. What is required is a combination of common-sense awareness and of experiential contact with the problem at hand. Though creativity in the realm of hypothesis is often in direct proportion to familiarity with the case, this situation does not invariably follow. Frequently the best hypotheses emerge only after we have given the mind a rest, allowing the subconscious to function on a level of its own. Imagination and memory frequently function best, not when they are engaged in a dogged pursuit of the object of their search, but rather as the result of a certain free play. This is not to say, however, that induction is an open invitation to our imaginations to run wild. "Free play" in the realm of induction means a willingness to explore relevant hypotheses no matter how remote they may initially appear. It does not, on the other hand, allow that we be guided by imagination alone, as when we tend—in the solution of a problem—to proceed immediately to think either the worst or the best.

In view of what has been said thus far, it is important to consider some criteria which may help us to differentiate a good hypothesis from a bad one. In the first place, a good hypothesis must provide a relevant explanation. The facts must not only fit into an orderly theoretical framework, but also be made to blend with any new facts which might be relevant. A good hypothesis ties all relevant facts into a rational scheme, an explanation, at the same time that it allows for the development of new facts.

A good hypothesis has a wide scope—it can be applied to many cases. The general usefulness of a hypothesis is a good criterion to select one hypothesis rather than another. In this same respect, a good hypothesis will be verified indirectly by facts which do not come under its explanatory power. And finally, a hypothesis should be as simple as possible.

EXERCISE 13.3

A. Write two or three paragraphs on the role of hypothesis in scientific inquiry and investigation. Preferably cite examples from one of your textbooks in the physical, biological, or social sciences.
B. Read a detective story that you consider worthwhile; recount its main outlines and explain why in relation to the logic of induction you consider it a good story.
C. Explain the importance both of careful observation and of hypothesis with respect to each of the following examples.

1. A CASE OF SORE MUSCLES

Last semester I found that on some days when I got home from school my legs ached. I couldn't understand why this was happening.

At first I thought it was because of the long distances I had to walk, but I realized that, although I had to walk these distances every day, the aching did not follow each day but only on some days. I then noticed that on the days my legs ached I had been wearing shoes with poor support; however, when I wore shoes with good support every day, the aching persisted. After pursuing several other explanations, such as the fact that I had to climb four flights of stairs every day, I found that none would hold up under examination.

Suddenly I was hit by a new and enlightening clue to the cause of my mysterious malady: the aching occurred only on Tuesdays and Thursdays. Each Tuesday and Thursday I attended modern-dance class, in which we were required to do exercises, the majority of which made use of leg muscles almost entirely. Since my leg muscles had not been accustomed to such exercise and my leg muscles had not developed because I had not used those muscles before, I reasoned that modern dance must be the main cause of my aches, or at least a necessary part of the cause in conjunction with the other possibilities I had already explored. The following day I talked to my modern-dance instructor, who told me that in her experience she had known several cases similar to mine in which muscles were used that had not been used before, and this had caused, for a few months, aching after each time the muscles were used.

2. A COOL SPOT IN THE DESERT

The weather and climate of the desert of the Southwest are fascinating—particularly to an individual born and reared in the East. There are so many strange observations which can be made that one can spend countless hours without elaborate scientific equipment. One such observation has been made by the writer over the past two years. During the spring and summer, when daylight lasts into the evening, my sons and I ride our bicycles throughout our neighborhood, which is at a much lower elevation than most of the city. In fact, it drops an estimated thirty feet in half a mile.

Many times during the late evening I have noted that the air in this lower elevation is cooler than the air at the higher elevation. This difference is most noticeable near a large arroyo which winds its way across the desert from the high ground to the lower ground. In the winter this low area seems to have more frequent and more severe frosts than does the higher area. Friends who live at higher elevations many times reported no frost in their area when ours has been rather heavily frost-covered.

The cool air currents and heavy frosts led me to conclude that these are the reasons my neighbors and I have been unsuccessful in attempting to grow citrus trees. This hypothesis has since been confirmed by a horticulturist. The situation is most frustrating, since only half a mile away citrus trees produce a tasty crop of fruit. This is indeed a freakish trick played by the desert climate.

FALLACIES OF INDUCTION

Hasty induction involves a premature assumption that a given hypothesis is true prior to an examination of alternative methods of explanation. One of its commonest variations is the fallacy of *hasty generalization,* which involves an overly ready leap from the "some" to the "all."

Examples:

1. Student A tried to find out whether he should take Professor Y's course in history. Since he is concerned about getting a good teacher, at random he asks the opinion of three students who have taken a course from Professor Y. Each of them agrees that Professor Y, although he requires much in the way of assignments, is a poor teacher. Student A decides to sign up for a different course.

> *Comment:* Although the opinion of the three students may be sound, Student A should make further inquiries or at least try to determine whether the three students in question were being fair-minded, what their own academic status is, and so on. He is too quick in formulating his decision.

2. The wife of an affluent businessman has been murdered, and the police are summoned to the scene of the crime. Without investigating the background of the husband and others who may have been involved, the police line up the usual list of suspects and conclude that one of them—a man with a beard, who was living in that section of the city at the time of the murder—is the presumed perpetrator of the crime.

> *Comment:* As is frequently the case, the attempt to "get a murder solved" or to "get it off the books" leads to an instance of hasty induction.

A second type of inductive fallacy is that of *post hoc ergo propter hoc.* This fallacy is more often than not the result of hasty induction and may therefore more properly be considered as special instance of hasty induction. It is based on the presumption that, because of a connection between two events in a given time sequence, they are causally related to each other. Suppose that you get the flu after going to the movies with a date, and you blame your date for the flu. Because one event (getting the flu) followed another, you immediately *assume* that the event which preceded it (being with your date) was the *cause* of your getting the flu.

Examples:

1. Every time I go to the grocery store with my wife, I notice that the bill is larger than when I go by myself.

> *Comment:* The case needs to be investigated. Your wife may or may not be the cause of the larger bill—as other factors not related to the presence of your wife may be the cause.

2. Every time I go with you to the horseraces, I lose. So you must be the cause of my losing.

> *Comment:* If your companion is in the habit of giving you bad tips

and you are in the habit of following them, then perhaps he is partially to blame. Otherwise, however, he may be an innocent bystander having nothing to do with your bad luck.

A third type of fallacy is that of *culpable omission,* sometimes known also as *forgetful induction.* This mistake consists of the failure to consider factors relevant to the solution of the particular problem. Suppose, for example, that you are taking a political poll as to which candidate is likely to win the next election. Instead of taking a "fair sampling" of different types of individuals from different locales, you restrict yourself to one type—let us say, to a group of affluent businessmen at a downtown hotel. The culpable omission here consists of your failure to vary the types.

Examples:

1. Although I am much more careful than my neighbor about watering my lawn, I consistently get poorer results than he does. Though he waters less, his lawn always seems to be green, while mine has a dried-out appearance.

   Comment: This might be a good opportunity for someone to come on with a commercial for the use of fertilizer.

2. The motor of your car stops, and you think that something has gone wrong with it. After much trouble you find that you simply ran out of gas.

   Comment: This type of situation is frequently an occasion for profanity.

EXERCISE 13.4

A. Name the fallacy and comment.

1. "Two prominent physical scientists predicted a few years ago that the polar icecaps were melting and that major coastal cities should begin now to plan for seawalls to protect themselves from the rising oceans. The predictions were based on scientific measurements of the size of icecaps and historical measurements of sea level over the past several hundred years. And the measurements were accurate. There was no fabrication. The world's icecaps were indeed melting and the world's oceans were indeed rising. But the authors did not tell the whole story. They neglected to emphasize that, in the long run, increased rainfall on land areas and accumulated snowfall in polar regions would tend to balance the effects of melting icecaps" (John H. Moore, "Assault From the Left: A Marxian Critique," *Revolution in America,* Vol. 5, No. 37, p. 35).

2. Each one of the coeds I met in this school (perhaps ten of them in all), though pretty, seems to have a low IQ. It must be that they're all this way, because meeting ten stupid coeds in a row cannot be a matter of mere coincidence. The law of averages is against it.

3. Every time I bake a cake for my husband, it looks and tastes terrible. It must be that doing it for him makes me nervous.

4. Our candidate, Milkie, is bound to win the next election hands down. He's the only one who appeals to the workers.

5. The three boys of your family whom I've met are all very polite. I can only suppose that the other nine are just as well-mannered.

THE ARGUMENT FROM ANALOGY

Much of the work of induction is based on an attempt to solve a problem by way of analogy—the drawing up of a comparison between one situation and another. Our treatment of the subject of analogy will include the use of analogy both as part of an inductive procedure and as a method of producing an argument, whether it is intendedly inductive or not.

It is misleading, of course, to suppose that there is any "stock" argument from analogy, since there are analogies of various sorts. However, since *every analogy is based on some type of comparison,* the validity of any given analogy will depend upon the *aptness and relevancy of the comparison* that is made.

For example, City X may decide that *because* a system of one-way streets has proved helpful in the downtown area of its neighbor, City Y, it should *therefore* adopt the same system. Here we have an example of an analogy that may or may not prove useful—depending, that is, upon a careful evaluation of a variety of circumstances, such as the comparative rate of traffic, its density, and the overall size of the area. However, it would be extremely naive for City X *without investigating the peculiarities of its own situation* to proceed uncritically on the basis of what its neighbor has done.

In general, there can be no set logical prescription for the valid use of the argument from analogy. This holds true especially in view of the fact that most analogies—to be helpful—require an intimate experiential knowledge of all the relevant data. The basic use of analogy, however, is relatively easy to grasp, as in the example that follows.

Example:

Recently a case was reported of a woman who twice had her skull opened surgically because she had all the indications of brain tumor. None was found. Investigation proved that her symptoms were produced by long-term, self-prescribed use of Vitamin A for a purpose which she herself had forgotten. Recent federal investigation has brought to light serious, even fatal, results from the use of some weight-reduction drugs, largely self-prescribed or continued without medical supervision.

Tranquilizers, stimulants, and reducing agents are particularly prone to unfavorable side effects. Many such medications damage the blood-forming systems, the liver, the central nervous system, the eyes, the ears, the skin. The damage they do may become irreversible. The list of sad side effects from self-prescribed use of drugs commonly found in the bathroom cabinet could be extended indefinitely. A frequent mistake is the unprescribed use of some leftover medicine that Sister Kate or Aunt Agatha had been taking for "something like what *I* seem to have." "It worked for her, so why not for me," is the reasoning.

This example highlights the danger of the unadvised use of the argument from analogy which is based on the unwarranted and untested supposition that what is good in one instance must be good in another. In the above example there are also undertones of the assumption, faultily applied, that "you can never get enough of a good thing." (Glance back at the unprescribed use of Vitamin A.)

Such expressions as *"a pari," "a fortiori,"* and *"a·minore"* are typical introductions to an argument from analogy. Thus an *a pari* argument from analogy signifies that what is true in one case is at least *equally* true in another (and perhaps also for the same reason). An *a fortiori* argument is one which claims that there is *all the more reason* for something being true, more advisable, and so on, as in another case or situation. Thus it may be argued that if one foreign country which is a *neutral* has received aid from the United States, then there is *all the more reason* why another which happens to be our *ally* should receive an even greater amount. Finally, an *a minore* argument is in a sense the reverse of the one just illustrated: it is a negative type of argument which defends the claim that there is *less reason* for doing or saying something in one case than in another. The following remark illustrates the point:

> (*Scene:* Two children in the rear seat of their father's
> car as he drives them through a desert area.)
> *Little girl:* John, we're in the "middle of nowhere."
> *Little boy:* Cathy, there's no such *place* as "nowhere." So you'll *never* find
> a place called the *middle* of nowhere.

The last type of argument is often introduced by the expression, "There is less reason to suppose . . . ."

EXERCISE 13.5

A. Examine the analogy employed in the following newspaper editorial.

> More than a century ago hardy pioneers who were in the vanguard of the westward movement of civilization were crying "California or bust." Today, in much the same vein, another breed of pioneers is saying "to the moon or bust." Like all pioneers, those in the space program face extremely difficult problems which at times make them ask themselves if the effort is worth the reward. . . . From the military and national security standpoint, space is the high ground of the cosmos, and no nation can afford to ignore it. The United States must excel in this respect. Today we have to some extent faltered on the space program, unfortunately. It is reflected in the public mood and the lowering appropriations.
>
> Perhaps the pioneers of a little more than a century ago also faltered, wondering if the journey on which they were embarking was worth the perils and cost. A look at the United States today answers that question with an emphatic "yes." Yesterday's pioneers were conquering *earth,* and their rewards were great. Today we are talking about conquering infinity, and the rewards are proportionately greater. As a nation, the United States cannot afford not to spend what is necessary to keep our supremacy in space (excerpted from *The San Diego Union,* July 30, 1967, p. C-2).

B. Examine the following arguments.

1. One of the problems with democracy in the United States is that the people themselves do not have a more direct share in the affairs of their government. In Switzerland, however, they do. What is wrong with democracy in the United States?
2. If a country like Japan can establish a system of world trade, why can't some of the backward countries of South America do the same thing?
3.

Professor Jones: You physicians are members of one of the highest-paid professions in the United States.

Dr. Winnowsmith: That may be so, but are you complaining about your university salary?

Professor Jones: You bet I am. I spent just as many years in preparation for my profession as you did for yours, and I receive only half the pay.

Dr. Winnowsmith: I grant that, and I think professors should receive higher pay. But I don't agree with your argument, because

professors don't do as much for society as physicians
do. If a man is in poor health, he'll pay anything to be
cured, and nobody blames him. So why shouldn't we
require higher fees?

Professor Jones: The analogy does not hold. A man's services to society
do not depend on the need of the patient to recognize
their worth. Few of my students recognize my worth,
but that doesn't make me useless.

Dr. Winnowsmith: That's true, but I have to serve my patients at all hours
of the day and night, and I work summers as well as
winters. Can you equal that performance?

Professor Jones: Again you are introducing false points of analogy, and
besides that, I guess you never see me burning the
midnight oil at home.

Dr. Winnowsmith: Look, Jones, we've been good friends and neighbors
for years. Let's forget the whole business of salaries
and go out and have a cup of coffee.

Professor Jones: Glad to, but you'll have to buy the coffee. I'm broke.

SUMMARY

By way of summary and conclusion we should note that the logic of
induction is "logic" in a sense only analogous to the meaning of that term
as applied to the different types of formal inference. Thus, in spite of the
fact that there are certain basic "canons" of induction (for example, of the
sort set forth in Mill's Methods), induction itself is not per se a formalized
method of procedure. Accordingly, the methods of induction are not such
that they can be determined and regulated by a *formal* set of rules, the
mere application of which would infallibly lead to the attainment of certain
definite results.

Indeed, the success of inductive procedures depends very largely on
such nonstandardized factors as a precise determination of the circumstances
relevant to the phenomenon at hand, the setting up of "working" hypotheses, and the testing of these hypotheses by the use of different types of
experiment. None of these procedures is such that it can be prescribed by
logical rule—as one can prescribe, for example, the rules of the syllogism.
As a result, the success of induction is as much dependent upon the practi-
tioner's powers of observation, his familiarity with the subject matter under
investigation, his ability to construct creatively certain fruitful hypotheses,
and his use of experiment to verify them as it is dependent on his "powers
of reasoning."

Finally, in any contrast that is drawn between the methods of deduction and the methods of induction one should always keep in mind the fact that in their actual use there is a constant interplay of *both* methods. Thus it is that (scientific) induction most often supplies us with premises from which we reason deductively. A scientist, for instance, by applying an inductive principle (a true universal) can often predict deductively the occurrence of a future event—for example, an eclipse. On the other hand, deduction plays a vital role as part of the general process of inductive inquiry, and that very largely in the elimination of nonsuccessful hypotheses.

The following example is provided as a model for further study and analysis.

The Case of the Tropical Fish

Since I have always been interested in tropical fish, this summer I bought a modest tank and stocked it with guppies, neon tetras, swordtails, and zebras, as well as with scavengers and several water plants. For a few months my tank was thriving and seemed to have attained a good ecological balance. But in November my fish began dying one by one, and I tried to determine the cause. The fish showed no symptoms other than slow growth, lack of sexual activity, and general torpidity.

I ruled out disease as a probable cause because the fish showed no symptoms other than those mentioned (and most common aquarium diseases have striking symptoms) and because the cause of death was not as selective as disease usually is: I lost at least one of each type of fish in the tank.

Having determined that the cause of death was probably environmental, I experimented with the variable factors in the tank. I varied both the amount and kind of food I had been using; I changed the water and cleaned the filter more often than usual; I trimmed back the water plants to prevent their decay and to allow more light in the tank. None of these remedies seemed to have any effect—the fish kept dying.

Finally I thought of the water temperature as a possible cause of death, and I received tentative confirmation of this hypothesis when I read in my *Aquarium Guide* that temperatures below 70 degrees are injurious to the health of most tropical fish. The guide further stated that cold water causes a slowing of metabolic processes, resulting in torpidity, lessened sexual activity, and slow growth. Since my fish had these symptoms and since their death had roughly coincided with the onset of cold weather, I accepted the water temperature as the probable cause of death.

The following day I bought and installed an aquarium heater, setting it at 76 degrees. I bought the heater in December, and I have lost only one fish since then. Furthermore, the symptoms began to diminish almost immediately and have not returned. I conclude, therefore, that my reasoning was correct and that cold water caused the death of my fish.

Observations

    A. Variety of tropical fish.
    B. Increased mortality rate in November.
    C. No unusual symptoms except general state of torpor.

Hypotheses and Testing of Hypotheses

    A. Disease. Ruled out (cause of death was not as selective as are most types of disease—at least one of each type of fish was lost.)
    B. Environmental Cause
        1. Food. Varied amount and kind of food: no significant change.
        2. Changed water and cleaned filter. No significant change.
        3. Trimmed water plants to allow more light in tank. No significant change.
        4. Water temperature. Tentative confirmation of hypothesis: information in *Guide Book*.
            a. Minimum required temperature is 70 degrees.
            b. Period of year (November).
            c. Installation of heater to bring water to 76 degrees.
            d. Return to normal activity; no more deaths.
            e. Cause of previous deaths: coldness of water
               (below 70 degrees).

Solution

    Use heater to keep water warm.

Symbolic Logic

A Formal Approach[1]

In this section we shall approach symbolic logic from a more rigorous point of view. Some of the most fundamental concepts of modern logic will be examined, and we shall see how these are employed in the explication of deductive inference. Through analysis of the concept of implication, we shall note how the logician departs from the ordinary language of statements. Finally, several important concepts will shed some light on the more complicated tools employed by the modern logician.

TRUTH FUNCTIONS

As has already been noted, sentences serve many different functions in our language. We use sentences to describe, to evoke feelings, to persuade, and so on. Strictly speaking, not all sentences can be true or false.

---

[1] At the discretion of the instructor the present chapter may or may not be omitted depending on the time limits and objectives of the course. This chapter may be considered as an extension and as a more formalized approach to some of the material presented in Chapter 12 on conditional and other types of hypothetical syllogisms.

For example, it is meaningless to speak of the sentence, "Shut the door!" as being either true or false. Our sole concern in this chapter will be with sentences to which it makes sense to attribute truth or falsity. Bearing in mind what we have already discussed in the first two chapters, the following is a stipulative definition: *A proposition is a sentence which expresses something that is either true or false.* The following are propositions:

1. Thales was a shrewd entrepreneur.
2. The *Titanic* hit an iceberg and sank.
3. The sun is 93,000,000 miles away from earth.

All of the above propositions differ in meaning. The first expresses something about Thales, the second says something about the *Titanic,* and the third makes an assertion about the sun. But they all have something in common: they are true. Examine now the following propositions:

1. Abraham Lincoln was the first president of the United States.
2. Trieste is in Sweden.
3. Alexander the Great was the tutor of Aristotle.

All of these propositions also differ in meaning; yet they all have something in common: each of them is false. Lincoln was the sixteenth president, Trieste is in Italy, and it was Aristotle who was the tutor of Alexander. We can therefore draw the following conclusion: all propositions are either true or false.

We are now ready to analyze propositions more closely. Generally speaking, propositions are either *simple* or *compound.* A compound proposition is one which can be analyzed (broken up) into at least two simple ones. A simple proposition cannot be further analyzed in terms of other propositions. Thus the proposition "Gold is yellow and lions are felines" is compound. It can be analyzed into the two propositions: "Gold is yellow" and "Lions are felines." But the proposition, "Gold is yellow" is simple because it cannot be broken down any further.

If it is the case that every proposition is either true or false, then every proposition will have a *truth value.* If a proposition is true its truth value is *true,* and if a proposition is false its truth value is *false.* Thus the truth value of the proposition "The earth is spherical in shape" is *true;* while the truth value of the proposition "Galileo wrote the *Critique of Pure Reason*" is *false.*

In the sense that simple propositions are not made up of other propositions, they do not depend on other propositions for their truth value. Compound propositions may either depend on their component propositions for their truth value or they may not. Compound propositions which do not depend on their component propositions for their truth value usually entail expressions of desire, belief, and the like. We shall not deal with such propositions here. *Our sole concern in what follows will be with compound propositions whose truth value depends only on the truth value of their components.* In this sense, since the truth value of a compound proposition will depend on the truth value of its components, the compound proposition will be a *function* of its components; or, more simply, a *truth function.* In other words, the truth value of a compound proposition will be determined exhaustively by the truth value of its component propositions. The following definition is therefore recommended:

> *A compound proposition is a truth function if, and*
> *only if, its truth or falsity is a function of the truth*
> *or falsity of its component propositions.*

From this it follows that the truth or falsity of the components *completely determine* the truth value of the compound proposition.

NEGATION

The negation of any proposition is the denial of its truth value. If the truth value of a proposition is true, then the truth value of its negation will be false. On the other hand, if the truth value of a proposition is false, then the truth value of its negation will be true. Usually the negation of a proposition is expressed by placing the word "not" in the correct place. The following is an example of a proposition and various ways of negating it:

Proposition	Ways of Negating it
All parrots speak English.	Not all parrots speak English. All parrots do not speak English. Some parrots do not speak English.

When we negate, we are reversing the truth value of the original proposition. Logicians usually make use of the symbol "$\sim$" to represent negation. Since the symbol changes the truth value of a proposition, it is called a *truth-functional operator.* If p is any proposition, then its negation is expressed as $\sim p$.[2] Since p can be either true or false, its negation can be either true or false. Thus if we negate the proposition $\sim p$ we obtain p. Let-

---

[2] Logicians make use of small (lower-case) letters (usually from the middle of the alphabet) to denote types of propositions. Capital letters usually denote specific propositions.

ting T or F stand for the truth value of any proposition p, the respective negation of p in terms of its truth value can be represented as follows:

$$\sim(T) = F \quad \text{and} \quad \sim(F) = T$$

It is convenient to express relationships of truth values by means of truth tables. If p is any proposition, then its negation may be represented as follows:

p	$\sim p$
T	F
F	T

It is helpful to notice that if a proposition is negated an even number of times, its truth value will not change. The following table makes this explicit:

p	$\sim p$	$\sim\sim p$	$\sim\sim\sim p$	$\sim\sim\sim\sim p$
T	F	T	F	T
F	T	F	T	F

From the above truth table it is clear that the truth values of columns 3 and 5 are the same as the truth value of the original proposition p.

CONJUNCTION

Given any two propositions, they may be linked by the word "and." The resulting compound proposition is called a *conjunctive proposition*, or *conjunction* for short. The two propositions connected by the word "and" are called *conjuncts*. Thus the proposition "A pool table has six pockets and a billiard table has no pockets" is a conjunction. Its two conjuncts are the simple propositions "A pool table has six pockets" and "A billiard table has no pockets." Logicians use the symbol " · " to represent the word "and." We need not restrict ourselves to the connection of only two propositions: the symbol " · " can connect as many propositions as we desire. In ordinary language other words serve to connect propositions in the same manner that "and" does. We can see this by examining the following conjunctions:

1. Although Aristotle was the pupil of Plato, he did not accept the Platonic Theory of Ideas literally.
2. Solidified carbon dioxide is cold, yet it burns.

3. Fermat and Gauss were mathematicians, but Beethoven was a composer.

The conjuncts of the above conjunctions are connected by the words "although," "yet," and "but" respectively. All words which connect in this manner can be considered to function as the " · " symbol. And since the symbol connects two conjuncts, thereby forming a truth-functional compound proposition, it is called a *truth-functional connective.* Attention should be given to the last proposition above, where the word "and" does not serve to connect two conjuncts, since the phrase "Fermat and Gauss" is considered as the whole subject, of which "mathematicians" is predicated. In other words, the word "and" does not connect two conjuncts: it serves to connect two names, which are the subject of the first conjunct, "Fermat and Gauss were mathematicians."

We are now in a position to analyze the truth value of a conjunction in terms of the truth value of its conjuncts. If we examine the conjunction "William Faulkner wrote *The Bear* and James Joyce wrote *Finnegans Wake,*" we see that it is made up of two conjuncts. In terms of truth value, these conjuncts can be related in four possible ways: the first can be true and the second one true, the first can be true and the second one false, the first can be false and the second one true, or both the first and second could be false. As we shall soon see, the only condition under which the conjunction is true is if both its conjuncts ("William Faulkner wrote *The Bear*" and "James Joyce wrote *Finnegans Wake*") are true.

If T or F are the only possible truth values that any two conjuncts may take, then their conjunction will have the following truth values as possibilities:

$$\cdot(T, T) = T \qquad \cdot(F, T) = F$$
$$\cdot(T, F) = F \qquad \cdot(F, F) = F$$

In terms of a truth table, the truth value of a conjunction can be fully determined by the truth values of its conjuncts. If $p \cdot q$ is any conjunction, and p and q are its respective conjuncts, then the truth values of the conjunction can be fully represented by the following truth table:

p	q	$p \cdot q$
T	T	T
T	F	F
F	T	F
F	F	F

It is clear from the above table that the truth value of the conjunction $p \cdot q$ is true (T) only if both conjuncts are true; in all other cases it is false. This holds no matter how complex the conjunction may be. If we had a conjunction made up of twenty conjuncts, then in order for that conjunction to be true, all of its twenty conjuncts would have to be true. If only one of them was false, then the whole conjunction would be false.

Thus far in our discussion, the symbols " $\sim$ " and " $\cdot$ " have been developed. Before continuing, it is important to translate ordinary English expressions into symbolic notation and to know the proper use of the symbols. Let us analyze some examples. Suppose we were given the following proposition: "It is not true that all Russians are Communists." In order to represent it symbolically, we let R stand for "All Russians are Communists." But since we have to negate it, the full symbolic representation becomes $\sim R$. Suppose, on the other hand, that we were given the proposition "Albert Camus died in a car accident." To represent it symbolically, we simply let any letter stand for the whole proposition—such as A. If we wish to negate it, then we simply write $\sim A$; and if we want to negate the negation of A, we get $\sim \sim A$, which is the same as our original proposition A.

To symbolize conjunctions we follow an analogous procedure. Suppose that we wanted to symbolize the conjunction "Bob went to the dance and Sue went shopping." To translate it into symbolic notation, we arbitrarily pick B to stand for the conjunct "Bob went to the dance" and S to stand for the conjunct "Sue went shopping." If we then let " $\cdot$ " take the place of "and," the symbolic expression $B \cdot S$ is the perfect translation of the original.

Looking back at our previous conjunction, $B \cdot S$, suppose that we wanted to negate it. In order to do this, we simply place the conjunction in parenthesis and place the negation symbol to the left of it. Our original expression, $B \cdot S$, then becomes $\sim (B \cdot S)$. Analysis in terms of a truth table gives the following results:

B	S	$B \cdot S$	$\sim (B \cdot S)$
T	T	T	F
T	F	F	T
F	T	F	T
F	F	F	T

Notice that we begin with the smallest expression. Thus, in order to get truth values for $\sim (B \cdot S)$, we first had to get truth values for $B \cdot S$. The truth values for $\sim (B \cdot S)$ were obtained by simply negating the truth values of $B \cdot S$ in the third column. It is to be noted that negating the whole conjunction is not equivalent to negating each of the conjuncts individually.

Thus, to negate each of the conjuncts of $B \cdot S$, we have to place a negation symbol in front of each of them. The new symbolic expression would then become $\sim B \cdot \sim S$, which, when translated into words, means, "It is not true that Bob went to the dance and it is not true that Sue went shopping." The truth table for $\sim B \cdot \sim S$ is the following:

B	S	$\sim B$	$\sim S$	$\sim B \cdot \sim S$
T	T	F	F	F
T	F	F	T	F
F	T	T	F	F
F	F	T	T	T

It is obvious, if we compare the two truth tables above, that negating the whole conjunction is not equivalent to negating each of the conjuncts separately. Under the negation of the whole conjunction we have the top value of the column as F, while all the rest are T. On the other hand, under the conjunction of the negations of the conjuncts, each of the first three values is an F, while the last value is a T.

Let us now determine the truth value of a more complicated conjunction. Suppose that K, L, M are true and U, V, W are false in the following proposition:

$$\sim[(K \cdot V) \cdot \sim L] \cdot [(M \cdot \sim U) \cdot \sim (W \cdot K)]$$

Beginning with the left expression, we see that if K is true and V is false, then their conjunction will be false. Since L is true, then $\sim L$ will be false. Now the conjunction of something false with something false is going to be false. Thus the expression within the brackets on the left side has the truth value of F; but since we have a negation sign in front of it, the whole expression becomes true. We work out the right side in the same manner. Since M is true and U is false, the conjunction of M with $\sim U$ will be true. Since W is false and K is true, their conjunction will be false, but since there is a negation sign in front of it, the expression becomes true. Since the right side is the conjunction of two true propositions, it is true. Thus, since both the lefthand and righthand expressions are true, their conjunction must also be true. Therefore, the whole proposition is true. Conventions to keep in mind:

1. The negation of any proposition changes its truth value.
2. A conjunction is true if all its conjuncts are true; in all other cases it is false.
3. The negation symbol operates on the smallest proposition which the symbolism allows.

4. The symbol " · " always connects two propositions.

5. The conventional use of brackets is as follows: $\left\{\,[\,(\,)\,]\,\right\}$

EXERCISE 14.1

A. Translate the following expressions into symbolic notation:

1. It is not the case that monkeys like bananas, although they often drink banana juice.
2. Aristophanes wrote good comedies, but Plato did not laugh, and my uncle cries, although my cousin Ferdinand and my aunt Felicia are indifferent.
3. Descartes did not write his *Meditations* in English.
4. Although some parallel lines meet in Riemannsville, and some triangles are greater than a half-circle, most Euclidean minds cannot understand these axioms.
5. Robert and Jennifer went to the park, but I stayed in the library.
6. Although I see her every day, I have never spoken to her and feel embarrassed when she comes near, yet I love her.

B. Mark each of the following expressions which are not well-formed with an N, and place a W in front of those that are well-formed:

1. $\sim p \cdot q$
2. $(p \cdot q \cdot r) \cdot (s \cdot \sim t) \cdot \sim p \cdot q$
3. $r \cdot (\sim p \cdot q)$
4. $\sim\sim p \cdot r \cdot (\sim\sim\sim p \cdot q)$
5. $(r \cdot s \cdot q \cdot t) \cdot \sim (p \cdot s \cdot r \cdot \sim x \sim v)$
6. $(p \cdot q) \sim \cdot r$
7. $(p \sim q) \cdot r$
8. $\sim\sim\sim\sim\sim\sim\sim\sim p \cdot (q \cdot s) \cdot r \cdot \sim (s \cdot \sim\sim\sim\sim\sim\sim\sim h)$
9. $p \cdot \sim q \sim$

C. Construct truth tables for the following types of propositions:

1. $\sim p \cdot q$
2. $p \cdot \sim q$
3. $p \cdot q \cdot r$
4. $\sim (p \cdot q) \cdot \sim p$
5. $p \cdot \sim p$
6. $(p \cdot q) \cdot (\sim p \cdot \sim q)$
7. $\sim p \cdot (\sim r \cdot p)$
8. $\sim q \cdot \sim p$

D. Assuming that K, L, M are true and U, V, W are false, what is the truth value of each of the following propositions?

1. $K \cdot L \cdot M \cdot \sim W$ 2. $\sim[(W \cdot \sim V) \cdot K] \cdot [\sim U \cdot (L \cdot V)]$
3. $(\sim V \cdot \sim U) \cdot (K \cdot L)$ 4. $\sim U \cdot L$
5. $\sim \sim K \cdot (\sim \sim \sim W \cdot L)$ 6. K

DISJUNCTION

Many times two or more propositions will be connected in the form of alternatives. The two propositions "The sun is shining" and "The wind is blowing" can be combined by inserting the word "or" in the appropriate place. The resulting compound proposition, "Either the sun is shining or the wind is blowing," is called a *disjunctive proposition* (*disjunction* for short). Disjunctions are also truth-functional in that they depend on their component propositions for their truth value. Logicians use the symbol "$\vee$" (called a *wedge*) to represent the disjunction of any two propositions. Generally speaking, disjunction is an "either/or" type of statement.

If we examine the above disjunctive proposition, we see that it would be true in case any one of the following conditions hold:

1. In case the sun were shining.
2. In case the wind were blowing.
3. In case both the sun were shining and the wind were blowing.

It is clear from the above example, that the minimum requirement for a disjunction to be true, is that *at least one of its disjuncts be true*. There is a minimum requirement but no maximum specification—if one disjunct is true, the whole disjunction will be true. This is why logicians call this particular sense of "or" *nonexclusive*. If one of the disjuncts is true, it does not exclude the possibility of other disjuncts' being true at the same time. From this it follows that a disjunction would only be false when all of its disjuncts are false. In all other cases it would be true.

Analogously to our consideration of conjunction, if we let T and F stand for the two possible truth values of the disjuncts of a disjunction, four possibilities emerge: both disjuncts can be true, the first can be true and the second one false, the first can be false and the second one true, or both can be false. Formally, we may represent these truth values thus:

$$v(T, T) = T \qquad v(T, F) = T$$
$$v(F, T) = T \qquad v(F, F) = F$$

If $p \vee q$ is any disjunction, then its respective truth values in terms of its disjuncts (p and q) can be represented by the following truth table:

p	q	$p \vee q$
T	T	T
T	F	T
F	T	T
F	F	F

Since in terms of truth values, the disjunction is exhaustively determined by its disjuncts, it can be understood as defining the "v" symbol.

There is also another use of "or," which logicians call the *exclusive* sense, which has both a minimum and a maximum requirement. Thus, given any two disjuncts p and q, if the "or" which combines them into a disjunction is used in the exclusive sense, then the meaning of the disjunctive proposition will be "either p or q, but not both." For example, if an employer says to a prospective employee, "We pay either $150.00 per week or $3.00 an hour," it is evident that if the person in question accepts the job, he will either get $150.00 per week or $3.00 an hour, *but not both*. This sense of "or" does not require a new symbol: we can easily represent it with the symbolism thus far developed. If p and q are the two disjuncts of the disjunction, $p \vee q$, then what we wish to symbolize is p or q, but not both. We symbolize *"p or q"* as $p \vee q$; and we can represent "both p and q" by $p \cdot q$. Then in order to represent the "not," we negate $p \cdot q$, and thus get $\sim(p \cdot q)$. Thus our final symbolic expression for the exclusive sense of "or" becomes:

$$(p \vee q) \cdot \sim(p \cdot q)$$

It is also easy to see that the exclusive disjunction of p and q asserts that at least one disjunct is true and at least one is false. This can be expressed as

$$(p \vee q) \cdot (\sim p \vee \sim q)$$

The expression $(p \vee q) \cdot \sim(p \cdot q)$ is equivalent to the expression $(p \vee q) \cdot (\sim p \vee \sim q)$. To see this, all we have to do is make up truth tables for both expressions and check their respective truth values. In order to make up a truth table for the first proposition, we break it down into all its components. The components of the proposition $(p \vee q) \cdot \sim(p \cdot q)$ are: p, q, $(p \vee q)$, $(p \cdot q)$, $\sim(p \cdot q)$, and finally, the whole compound proposition itself, $(p \lor q) \cdot \sim(p \cdot q)$. We represent the respective values of the components and the whole compound proposition as follows:

p	q	$p \lor q$	$p \cdot q$	$\sim(p \cdot q)$	$(p \lor q) \cdot \sim(p \cdot q)$
T	T	T	T	F	F
T	F	T	F	T	T
F	T	T	F	T	T
F	F	F	F	T	F

From the above table it is clear that the truth value of the last column is F when either p and q are both T or p and q are both F. The only time the truth value of $(p \lor q) \cdot \sim(p \cdot q)$ is T is when either p is T and q is F or when p is F and q is T. The truth value of the third column was obtained from the truth values of the first two; the truth value of the fourth column was obtained from the first two also; the truth value of the fifth column was obtained by negating the truth values of the fourth; and finally, the truth values for the last column were obtained from the third and fifth. In this formal manner we have brought out the full meaning of the exclusive sense of "or."

In the preceding paragraph we noted that the conjunctions $(p \lor q) \cdot \sim(p \cdot q)$ and $(p \lor q) \cdot (\sim p \lor \sim q)$ were equivalent. To verify this, let us now make up a truth table for $(p \lor q) \cdot (\sim p \lor \sim q)$.

p	q	$p \lor q$	$\sim p$	$\sim q$	$\sim p \lor \sim q$	$(p \lor q) \cdot (\sim p \lor \sim q)$
T	T	T	F	F	F	F
T	F	T	F	T	T	T
F	T	T	T	F	T	T
F	F	F	T	T	T	F

The truth tables show the truth values under the expression $(p \lor q) \cdot \sim(p \cdot q)$ to be the same as those under the expression $(p \lor q) \cdot (\sim p \lor \sim q)$. If two propositions have the same truth values, they are said to be equivalent. *Two propositions are equivalent if, and only if, they have corresponding truth values.* Thus the expression $(p \lor q) \cdot \sim(p \cdot q)$ is truth-functionally equivalent to the expression $(p \lor q) \cdot (\sim p \lor \sim q)$.

Looking at the same two truth tables once again, we see that the component $\sim(p \cdot q)$ of the first table has the same truth values as the component $\sim p \lor \sim q$ of the second table. Thus, according to our previous definition, $\sim(p \cdot q)$ is truth-functionally equivalent to $\sim p \lor \sim q$. This interesting relationship is known as one of De Morgan's Theorems.[3] The

---

[3] So named after Augustus De Morgan (1806–1871), English mathematician and logician who is today best remembered for his development of a new logic of rela-

other of his theorems says that $\sim(p \lor q)$ is truth-functionally equivalent to $(\sim p \cdot \sim q)$. Logicians use the symbol "$\equiv$" to represent this kind of equivalence. Using the new symbol for equivalence, we may express De Morgan's Theorems as follows:

I. $\sim(p \cdot q) \equiv (\sim p \lor \sim q)$
II. $\sim(p \lor q) \equiv (\sim p \cdot \sim q)$

In words, the first theorem says that the negation of the conjunction of two propositions is equivalent to the disjunction of their negation. The second theorem says that the negation of the disjunction of two propositions is equivalent to the conjunction of their negations. We can establish the equivalence of the two parts of the second theorem by the following truth table:

p	q	$p \lor q$	$\sim(p \lor q)$	$\sim p$	$\sim q$	$\sim p \cdot \sim q$
T	T	T	F	F	F	F
T	F	T	F	F	T	F
F	T	T	F	T	F	F
F	F	F	T	T	T	T

The above table clearly establishes that the truth values of the fourth column are the same as those of the last column. Thus the two expressions are equivalent.

At this point it is important to bear in mind that the symbol "$\lor$" is to be understood as representing the nonexclusive sense of "or." Suppose that we wanted to analyze the disjunction $(p \lor q) \lor \sim(q \lor p)$ by means of a truth table. We follow our established procedure of breaking the disjunction into its components before representing these by a truth table. The components of the above proposition are: p, q, $(p \lor q)$, $\sim(q \lor p)$, and finally, the whole disjunction. The following truth table makes the truth values explicit:

p	q	$p \lor q$	$\sim(q \lor p)$	$(p \lor q) \lor \sim(q \lor p)$
T	T	T	F	T
T	F	T	F	T
F	T	T	F	T
F	F	F	T	T

tions. Though De Morgan expounded these theorems, they were in fact first expressed by William of Occam, fourteenth-century English scholastic philosopher, who opposed Thomism by insisting that universals have no real existence and that logic therefore deals with signs, not with realities.

It is interesting to note that the truth values of $(p \lor q) \lor \sim (q \lor p)$ are all T's. When all the values of a proposition are T's, the proposition is called a *tautology*. The above disjunctive proposition is therefore a tautology.

Let us now, as an example, determine the truth value of a disjunction. Given that $K, L,$ and M are true and that $U, V,$ and W are false, what is the truth value of the disjunction, $[(W \cdot K) \lor \sim U \cdot (L \lor W)] \lor [K \cdot (L \lor M) \lor (V \cdot W) \cdot L]$? The following is a schematic representation of how the truth value is determined:

$$[(W \cdot K) \lor \sim U \cdot (L \lor W)] \lor [K \cdot (L \lor M) \lor (V \cdot W) \cdot L]$$

$$\begin{array}{c}
F \quad T \qquad T \quad F \qquad\qquad T \quad T \qquad F \quad F \\
F \qquad\qquad T \qquad T \qquad\qquad T \qquad T \qquad F \qquad T \\
\quad\qquad T \qquad\qquad\qquad\qquad T \qquad\qquad\qquad F \\
\qquad\qquad\qquad\qquad T \qquad\qquad\qquad\qquad\qquad T
\end{array}$$

The arrows indicate the progressive derivation of the truth value of the disjunction. We begin with the expressions represented by the shortest arrows and work our way through until the truth value of the whole disjunction represented by the longest arrow is obtained. Beginning on the left side, if W is F and K is T, then their conjunction will be F; if L is T and W is F, then their disjunction will be T. Since $\sim U$ is T (because U is F), then its conjunction with $(L \lor W)$ will be T, because $(L \lor W)$ is T. Thus, since we have an F under $(W \cdot K)$ but a T under $\sim U \cdot (L \lor W)$, then their disjunction will have to be a T. The reasoning on the righthand side is analogous. Since L is T and M is T, their disjunction will have to be T; and since this T is in conjunction with the T of K, then the whole expression becomes T. Now since V and W are both F, their conjunction will have to be F; and since L is T, then its conjunction with the F of $(V \cdot W)$ will have to be F. Still looking at the right side, we have a T on the left and an F on the right, and therefore the disjunction of the two expressions will have to be a T. Looking at the whole disjunction, we have a T on the left and a T on the right; therefore the disjunction of these two will have to be T. The truth value of the whole disjunction is therefore true.

EXERCISE 14.2

A. Using your own symbols, translate the following into symbolic notation:

1. It is not true that Donna and Dina came or that they were late.
2. The killer stared at the iron bars, and either self-pity invaded him or he cried because tomorrow he would be hanged.

3. Cassandra stayed home and Priscilla went to Dennisport, but James went either fishing or swimming.
4. Either summer follows spring, or autumn follows summer and winter follows autumn.
5. Love me or I'll die.
6. Either a picayunish example is ridiculously nefarious or some euphemisms are wickedly serious and dull.
7. "Not" can be more powerful than "nor," and "and" often leads to boredom, but either "neither" is neutral or "therefore" is deadly.

B. Assuming that K, L, and M are true and U, V, and W are false, determine the truth value of each of the following propositions:

1. $(K \vee L) \cdot (W \cdot M)$
2. $U \vee (\sim W \cdot \sim K)$
3. $(K \cdot V) \vee (W \vee L)$
4. $[(K \vee V \vee W) \cdot \sim L] \vee [(K \cdot L) \vee (W \cdot L)]$
5. $(\sim L \vee \sim W) \vee (L \vee W)$
6. $(K \cdot L \cdot M) \vee (U \vee V \vee W)$

TRUTH-FUNCTIONAL IMPLICATION

In dealing with conditionals in Chapter 11, we found that a conditional (or hypothetical) proposition was found to be true when its consequent actually followed from its antecedent. Where the antecedent is actualized and the consequent does not follow, the conditional is false. In this sense, the truth or falsity of a conditional depended on an empirical examination. For example, to find out whether the conditional "If sodium is placed in water, then hydrogen is liberated" is true, we have to test the proposition in the laboratory.

This section analyzes the concept of implication on a more formal basis. Analogously to our treatment of conjunction and disjunction, we may approach our analysis of implication by considering the question: In terms of the truth values of its components (antecedent and consequent), when is a conditional true and when is it false? To find an answer there is no need for empirical investigation: we shall simply analyze the truth value of the conditional in terms of the truth values of its components.

Let us examine the following conditional proposition:

If you eat candy, then you will become obese.

The antecedent (eating candy) and the consequent (becoming obese) can be related in four possible ways:

1. Both antecedent and consequent can be true.
2. The antecedent can be true and the consequent false.
3. The antecedent can be false and the consequent true.
4. Both antecedent and consequent can be false.

If the first possibility is the case, the hypothetical is true. If the second possibility is actualized, the hypothetical is clearly false.

The last two cases pose some difficulty, since their consideration involves a transition from our normal concept of implication to what logicians call *material implication*. Considering the third possibility, what is the truth value of the hypothetical if a person does *not* eat candy but becomes obese just the same? There is nothing queer about this possibility. The hypothetical says, *"If you eat candy, then you will become obese"*; it *does not say, "Only if . . . , then . . . ."* I could become obese by eating many other things. In other words, it is sufficient that I eat candy in order to become obese, but it is not necessary. In this sense, becoming obese without eating candy will not affect the truth of becoming obese by eating candy. Thus if it is true that "If you eat candy, then you will become obese," this truth will not be affected by the person's becoming obese from some other cause. Thus in terms of the third possibility, the hypothetical is true.

The last possibility has nothing to do with either eating candy or becoming obese. What, then, can we say about the truth value of the hypothetical in terms of this possibility? In a very obvious sense, we cannot say anything, for no matter what else we do, it will be irrelevant to the hypothetical in question. But by the same token, if we do anything else, this will not affect the truth of the hypothetical in question, if it is true. Thus if obesity does follow from eating candy, our doing anything else will not change that. And therefore we can say that in terms of the last possibility, our hypothetical will be true.

The four possible truth values of any hypothetical can be expressed as follows:

$$\supset (T,T) = T \qquad \supset (T,F) = F$$
$$\supset (F,T) = T \qquad \supset (F,F) = T$$

We should not take the symbol "$\supset$" to mean "implies" as we normally understand this term, for it is evident from the preceding analysis that there is a difference in the assignment of truth values between the first and last two possibilities. It makes sense to say of the first two cases that the "if . . . then" has force, whereas in the last two cases, this conclusion is not plausible. In other words, only in the first two cases do we have a relation of *real implication*. It is in the sense of considering the four possible truth values of any hypothetical that the symbol "⊃" departs from the ordinary meaning of implication to signify the concept of *material implication.*

If $p \supset q$ is the form of any hypothetical proposition, its possible truth values in terms of the truth values of its antecedent, p, and consequent, q, can be represented by the following truth table:

p	q	$p \supset q$
T	T	T
T	F	F
F	T	T
F	F	T

The correct application of the symbol "⊃" will depend solely on the terms of the definition established by the above truth table analysis. By a consideration of the table it is clear that since $p \supset q$ will be false only in the event that p is true and q is false, we can understand the *essential meaning* of $p \supset q$ as expressing the logical fact that the conjunction of p with $\sim q$ will not hold. Thus $p \supset q$ essentially states that we cannot have both p and $\sim q$. Symbolically, the import of $p \supset q$ can be expressed as $\sim(p \cdot \sim q)$. To see that these two expressions are equivalent, examine the following truth table:

p	q	$\sim q$	$p \supset q$	$p \cdot \sim q$	$\sim(p \cdot \sim q)$
T	T	F	T	F	T
T	F	T	F	T	F
F	T	F	T	F	T
F	F	T	T	F	T

The above table shows the truth values of the fourth column to be exactly the same as those of the last column. Therefore, the expression $p \supset q$ is truth-functionally equivalent to $\sim(p \cdot \sim q)$. Another way of saying this is that either we do not have p or we have q. In other words, either p is false or q is true. Therefore the following three expressions are equivalent and may be interchanged without change of truth value:

$$\sim p \vee q \equiv \sim(p \cdot \sim q) \equiv p \supset q$$

We determine the truth value of a hypothetical proposition analogously to the determination for disjunctions. Given that $K, L,$ and M are true and $U, V,$ and W are false, what would be the truth value of the hypothetical proposition, $(K \vee U) \supset (M \supset W)$? Beginning with the lefthand side, we see that if K is true and U is false, their disjunction will be true. With respect to the righthand side, if *M* is true and *W* is false, *M* ⊃ *W* will have to be false. Since the antecedent of the hypothetical is true and the consequent is false, the whole hypothetical proposition will be false. Thus the truth value of (*K* v *U*) ⊃ (*M* ⊃ *W*) is false.

The construction of truth tables for hypotheticals is also analogous to that of conjunction and disjunction. Suppose that we wanted to make a truth table for the proposition, (*S* v *R*) ⊃ (∼*S* ⊃ *R*). We break the proposition down into its components and then proceed. The components of the proposition are: *S, R, S* v *R,* ∼*S,* ∼*S* ⊃ *R,* and finally, the full hypothetical itself. A truth table analysis yields

S	*R*	*S* v *R*	∼*S*	∼*S* ⊃ *R*	(*S* v *R*) ⊃ (∼*S* ⊃ *R*)
T	T	T	F	T	T
T	F	T	F	T	T
F	T	T	T	T	T
F	F	F	T	F	T

In the above truth table, column three was obtained from the first two. The fourth column was obtained by negating the first. The fifth was determined from the fourth and second. Finally, the truth values of the last column were obtained from the third and fifth respectively.

EXERCISE 14.3

A. Construct truth tables for the following hypothetical propositions.

1. [*R* · (*S* v *R*)] ⊃ (*R* ⊃ *S*)
2. (*S* ⊃ *R*) ⊃ (*R* ⊃ *S*)
3. *R* ⊃ (*S* ⊃ *R*)
4. (*R* v *S*) ⊃ (*S* ⊃ *R*)
5. (*S* · *R*) ⊃ (*R* v *S*)
6. ∼(*R* v *S*) ⊃ (∼*R* · ∼*S*)

B. Translate the following into symbolic notation.

1. If the aroma of violets pervades the air, then spring is coming.
2. Joan will go if Mary does.
3. If there are five halogens, then either the heaviest is radioactive or the periodic table is a scandal.
4. Only if "z" is greater than "y" is "x" greater than "w."
5. If *precipitevolissimevolmente* is the longest word in Italian and *antidisestablishmentarianism* is the longest word in English, then Laputa is inhabited by mad mathematicians.

6. If at first you do not succeed, then try again or give up.

7. If Napoleon either suffered from megalomania or died of cancer, then either Kazantzakis wrote *Freedom or Death* or Dante died in Ravenna.

8. If logic improves the mind, then push-ups improve the body; and if logic does not improve the mind, then this exercise is a waste of time.

9. Only if Shakespeare wrote *Hamlet* and Dante is the author of *Vita Nuova* is Beethoven the creator of the *Third Symphony*.

10. If a bachelor is an unmarried male and an unmarried male is a bachelor, then the Morning Star is the Evening Star and the Evening Star is the Morning Star.

11. If it rains cats and dogs, then it pours; and if it pours, then it rains cats and dogs.

C. If K, L, and M are true, and U, V, and W are false, what is the truth value of each of the following propositions?

1. $(K \supset W) \cdot (V \vee M)$
2. $[(L \vee U) \supset M] \supset [(U \cdot W) \vee (K \supset V)]$
3. $(K \cdot L) \supset (\sim W \cdot \sim U)$
4. $[\sim L \supset (V \cdot K \cdot M)] \supset \sim[(K \vee V) \supset (M \cdot \sim U)]$
5. $K \supset \sim V$
6. $[(K \supset M) \supset (\sim U \sim V)] \supset [(\sim U \sim V) \supset (K \supset M)]$
7. $\sim V \supset \sim U$
8. $[(U \supset V) \cdot (V \supset W)] \supset [(K \supset L) \cdot (L \supset M)]$

TAUTOLOGIES, CONTRADICTIONS, AND CONTINGENT STATEMENTS

The statement, "Pirandello wrote *Henry IV*" happens to be true. But it need not have been true: someone else could have written the play. In this sense, the above statement is not necessary but *contingent*. Examine now the following statement:

Either Pirandello wrote *Henry IV* or he did not write it.

The preceding statement (or proposition) is necessarily true. A person need not know anything about Pirandello to know that he either wrote the play or did not write it. Such a statement is independent of matters of fact. Since it does not depend on empirical knowledge for its truth, it is called a *necessary statement,* or *tautology.* If we let P stand for "Pirandello wrote *Henry IV*," then we can symbolize "Either Pirandello wrote *Henry IV* or he did not write it" as $P \vee \sim P$. A truth-table analysis of $P \vee \sim P$ yields the following results:

P	$\sim P$	$P \vee \sim P$
T	F	T
F	T	T

It is clear from the above table that the truth values of $P \vee \sim P$ are all T. Any statement which has only true truth values is a tautology. To determine whether a statement is a tautology, we simply construct a truth table for it and check the truth values under it.

The following is an example of another important type of statement:

Pirandello wrote *Henry IV* and he did not write it.

The immediately preceding proposition is known as a contradiction. All such contradictions are necessarily false. If we let $P \cdot \sim P$ stand for the above conjunction, then a truth-table analysis will explicitly indicate that it is necessarily false.

P	$\sim P$	$P \cdot \sim P$
T	F	F
F	T	F

In examining the above truth table, we see that the proposition $P \cdot \sim P$ has only F's under it, demonstrating that it is a necessarily false proposition.

By constructing a truth table and examining the truth values of any proposition, we can easily determine whether it is a tautology,[4] a contradiction, or simply a contingent statement.

EXERCISE 14.4

By means of truth tables, determine whether the following are contradictions, tautologies, or contingent propositions:

1. $(P \vee \sim P) \cdot (\sim P \cdot P)$
2. $(P \vee R) \supset (R \vee P)$
3. $P \supset (P \supset Q)$
4. $(P \supset \sim Q) \supset \sim P$
5. $(\sim P \vee Q) \vee \sim Q$
6. $(P \supset Q) \cdot (\sim P \supset \sim Q)$

---

[4] Not all necessarily true statements are tautologies. For a discussion of this point, see Chapter 6.

VALIDITY

In discussing the difference between a proposition and an argument, we found that propositions are either true or false whereas arguments are either valid or invalid. In a valid argument the conclusion follows necessarily from the premises. Thus, given any argument, if it is valid, then the conclusion is a legitimate inference from the premises; if the conclusion does not follow, then the argument is invalid. Let us look at the following argument:

> Either Mason is a good pool player or he is very lucky.
> Mason is not a good pool player.
> Therefore, he is very lucky.

If we let *M* stand for "Mason is a good pool player" and *H* for "He is very lucky," we may express the above argument as follows:

$$M \vee H$$
$$\sim M$$
$$\overline{\therefore H}$$

The first premise of the above argument tells us that at least one component is true. The second premise tells us that one of the components (M) is false. The conclusion is that the other component (H) must be true. We may test the validity of this argument by the following truth table:

M	H	$\sim M$	$M \vee H$
T	T	F	T
T	F	F	T
F	T	T	T
F	F	T	F

We test for validity by checking the truth values under each premise and under the conclusion. *If we can find one case in which the premises are true and the conclusion false, that is enough to tell us that the argument is invalid.* If we do not find such a case, then the argument is valid. Cases in which one or more premises are false are irrelevant to our considerations. In order to test for validity, therefore, we look only at those rows which have true premises. Then we look at the corresponding (*same row*) conclusion, and if it is false, the argument is invalid. If we look at the above truth table, we see that the two premises ($\sim M$ and $M \lor H$) are true only in the third row. Therefore (in this case), this is the only row by which we can determine validity. It is our *guide row*. We then look at the corresponding (same row, but different column) conclusion and check its truth value. In this argument, the conclusion (H) is not false; therefore, the argument is valid.

The above argument is an example of a particular type of argument known as the *disjunctive syllogism*. This general type of argument may be expressed as

$$\frac{p \lor q}{\sim p} \quad \text{or} \quad \frac{p \lor q}{\sim q}$$
$$\therefore q \qquad\qquad \therefore p$$

The *propositional variables* (small letters) may be replaced by any proposition (capital letters). Thus, if for p and q we substitute M and H, we return to our original argument. Consider now the following argument:

> If Elizabeth is telling the truth, then Marge is not lying.
> If Marge is lying, then Lee is wrong.
> Either Marge is lying or Lee is wrong.
> Lee is not wrong.
> Therefore, Elizabeth is not telling the truth.

The above argument gives three main statements and their corresponding negations. The three statements are: "Elizabeth is telling the truth" (which we can symbolize as E), "Marge is lying" (M), and "Lee is wrong" (L). Since the other statements are simply negations of these, we do not need new letters to represent them: all that we have to do in order to represent them is to put a negation sign in front of their corresponding positive statements. The number of *different statements* (not counting their respective negations) will determine the number of rows of our truth table. Since each statement can have a possible truth value of either true or false, the truth value of any statement has two possibilities. But we must raise this possibility to the number of different statements given, in order to exhaust every possible combination. Our general rule for the determination of the number of rows of a truth table will therefore be 2^n, where "n" is the number of different statements. Two statements result in four rows; three statements (as above) will give eight rows; four statements require sixteen rows; and so on.

Symbolizing the above argument:

$E \supset \sim M$
$M \supset L$
$M \vee L$
$\sim L$
_____
$\therefore \sim E$

Since we have three different letters (excepting their negations), these standing for our three different statements, a truth-table analysis of the above argument will yield eight rows.

E	M	L	$\sim E$	$\sim M$	$\sim L$	$E \supset \sim M$	$M \supset L$	$M \vee L$
T	T	T	F	F	F	F	T	T
T	T	F	F	F	T	F	F	T
T	F	T	F	T	F	T	T	T
T	F	F	F	T	T	T	T	F
F	T	T	T	F	F	T	T	T
F	T	F	T	F	T	T	F	T
F	F	T	T	T	F	T	T	T
F	F	F	T	T	T	T	T	F

By examining the table we see that there is no guide row. That is, there is no row in which all the premises are true (so that we could verify if the conclusion is T or F). This means that we cannot find a row with all true premises and a false conclusion. Thus the argument cannot be invalid (in which case it must be valid). However the argument is peculiar in that its premises are *inconsistent*—which means that the conjunction of all the premises yields a contradiction. (As an exercise the student should verify this for himself). Any argument of the form

q
$- q$
_____
$\therefore r$

is always valid.

Another example is worth noting. Suppose that we wanted to determine the validity of the argument:

If tomorrow is the end of the world, then Bob will drink a beer.
Bob will drink a beer.
Therefore, tomorrow is the end of the world.

Letting E stand for "Tomorrow is the end of the world" and B for "Bob will drink a beer," we can symbolize the argument as

$$E \supset B$$
$$B$$
$$\overline{\therefore E}$$

A truth-table analysis yields

E	B	$E \supset B$
T	T	T
T	F	F
F	T	T
F	F	T

The first and third rows are our guides, for that is where all the premises (two in this case) are true. The first row says that the conclusion is true, and this would tend to support the fact that the argument might be valid. But if we carefully examine the third row, we see that the conclusion there is false. We have found one case of true premises with a false conclusion, and that is all we needed to show the argument to be invalid.

EXERCISE 14.5

A. Translate the following into symbolic notation and test for validity by means of the truth-table method.

1. If Peter is late, then he will miss the boat. If he misses the boat, the captain will not be pleased. Either the captain will be pleased or Peter will not miss the boat. Peter will miss the boat. Therefore, Peter will be late.
2. If you do not drink milk, then you do not have powerful bones. But you have powerful bones. Therefore, you drink milk.
3. Either you go or I go. If you do not go, then I do not go. Either you go or you do not go. So I go.
4. If a man is short or tall, then he will not be of average height. A man is either short or tall. Thus, no man is of average height.
5. If an army is triumphant, then it does not plunder the land. If an army is not triumphant, then it refrains from plundering the land. Now an army either is triumphant or it is not triumphant. It follows that no army plunders the land.

B. Determine whether the following arguments are valid or not.

1. $K \supset \sim N$
    $\sim K \supset \sim N$
    $\overline{}$
    $\therefore \sim N$

2. $\sim K \supset \sim U$
    $U \supset R$
    $\sim R$
    $\overline{}$
    $\therefore K$

3. L
    $\overline{}$
    $\therefore L \vee R$

4. $(R \supset M) \cdot (S \supset L)$
    $R \vee S$
    $\overline{}$
    $\therefore M \vee L$

5. S
    T
    $\overline{}$
    $\therefore S \cdot T$

6. $K \supset Z$
    $\sim Z$
    $\overline{}$
    $\therefore \sim K$

7. $(M \supset L) \cdot (O \supset K)$
    $\sim L \vee \sim K$
    $\overline{}$
    $\therefore \sim M \vee \sim O$

8. $R \vee S$
    R
    $\overline{}$
    $\therefore \sim S$

9. $\sim S \supset T$
    $T \supset \sim S$
    $\overline{}$
    $\therefore \sim S \supset \sim S$

WORKING WITH THE RULES OF INFERENCE

The truth-table method of testing for validity becomes awkward as the number of statements making up an argument increases. A more efficient way to determine the validity of an argument is to examine each step to see whether it can be justified by a rule of inference. Suppose that we wanted to check the validity of the following argument:

> If you are a good surfer, then you have been on a storm wave.
> If you have been on a storm wave, then you have heard the harp.
> Either you have not heard the harp or it was all a dream.
> It was not all a dream.
> Therefore, you are not a good surfer.

The above argument has four premises and a conclusion. To see whether the conclusion follows from the premises, let us first symbolize the argument. Picking arbitrary letters, we symbolize the first premise as $S \supset W$. The second premise is $W \supset H$. The third is $\sim H \vee D$. The last one is simply $\sim D$. And the conclusion is $\sim S$. We then number the symbolized premises and the conclusion in the following way:

1. $S \supset W$
2. $W \supset H$
3. $\sim H \vee D$
4. $\sim D$ $/ \therefore \sim S$

Simply by working with the premises, let us see if we can obtain the desired conclusion, $\sim S$. Since the third premise is $\sim H \vee D$, and the fourth one is $\sim D$, we can get $\sim H$ through the *disjunctive syllogism*. For a disjunctive syllogism says that of two alternatives, if one is not true, then the other one must be true. Since we now have $\sim H$, we must also have $\sim W$ by *modus tollens*. And since we now have $\sim W$, then we must also have $\sim S$ through *modus tollens*. Our valid argument, with each justified step would look like this:

1. $S \supset W$
2. $W \supset H$
3. $\sim H \vee D$
4. $\sim D$ $/\therefore \sim S$
5. $\sim H$ 4,3, Disjunctive Syllogism
6. $\sim W$ 5,2, *Modus Tollens*
7. $\sim S$ 6,1, *Modus Tollens*

Since $\sim S$ was derived from the given premises, the argument is valid. In any such argument we justify each step by a valid rule of inference. If we thus obtain our given conclusion, then our argument is valid.

We can use many other rules of inference to justify a step in an argument. The following are among the more important, and the student should familiarize himself with them:

1. $p \supset q$ *Modus Ponens*
   p $/\therefore q$
2. $p \supset q$ *Modus Tollens*
   $\sim q$ $/\therefore \sim p$
3. $p \vee q$ *Disjunctive Syllogism*
   $\sim p$ $/\therefore q$
4. p *Conjunction*
   q $/\therefore p \cdot q$
5. $p \cdot q$ $/\therefore p$ *Simplification of Conjunction*
6. p $/\therefore p \vee q$ *Addition*
7. $p \supset q$ *Chain Argument*
   $q \supset r$ $/\therefore p \supset r$
8. $(p \supset q) \cdot (r \supset s)$ *Constructive Dilemma (Complex)*
   $p \vee r$ $/\therefore q \vee s$
9. $(p \supset q) \cdot (r \supset q)$ *Constructive Dilemma (Simple)*
   $p \vee r$ $/\therefore q$
10. $(p \supset q) \cdot (r \supset s)$ *Destructive Dilemma (Complex)*
    $\sim q \vee \sim s$ $/\therefore \sim p \vee \sim r$
11. $(p \supset q) \cdot (p \supset r)$ *Destructive Dilemma (Simple)*
    $\sim q \vee \sim r$ $/\therefore \sim p$

The above types of argument are all valid, as may be confirmed by means of a truth table. Any one of the above types may be invoked to justify a step in any given argument. In the following argument the steps are justified by five of the above rules:

1.	$\sim(P \supset Q) \supset \sim F$	
2.	$\sim(R \supset S) \supset \sim D$	
3.	$F \cdot D$	
4.	$P \vee R$	
5.	$\sim S$	$/ \therefore Q$
6.	F	3, Simplification
7.	$P \supset Q$	1,6, Modus Tollens
8.	D	3, Simplification
9.	$R \supset S$	8,2 Modus Tollens
10.	$(P \supset Q) \cdot (R \supset S)$	7,9, Addition
11.	$Q \vee S$	4,10 Constructive Dilemma (Complex)
12.	Q	5,11 Disjunctive Syllogism

Notice that in the above argument there are five premises and a conclusion, Q. The conclusion was derived from the premises by steps which were justified by the above rules. Also observe that when we justify a step, we must tell where the step came from. Thus step ten, for example, was obtained from steps seven and nine by addition.

EXERCISE 14.6

Justify each step which is not a premise in the following arguments:

1.	$(A \supset B) \cdot (C \supset D)$		2.	$\sim(R \supset S) \supset \sim D$	
	$\sim A \supset Q$			$\sim(P \supset Q) \supset \sim F$	
	$F \supset \sim Q$			$F \cdot D$	
	$G \supset \sim R$			$P \vee R$	
	$F \cdot G$	$/ \therefore B \vee D$		$\sim S$	$/ \therefore Q$
	F			F	
	G			$P \supset Q$	
	$\sim Q$			D	
	$\sim R$			$R \supset S$	
	A			$\sim R$	
	$A \vee C$			P	
	$B \vee D$			Q	

3. $(R \cdot S) \supset \sim P$
   $\sim P \supset M$
   $U \vee \sim M$
   $\sim U$ $/ \therefore \sim (R \cdot S)$
   $\sim M$
   P
   $\sim (R \cdot S)$

4. $[(R \cdot S) \supset M] \cdot (W \supset M)$
   $\sim (R \cdot S) \supset P$
   $\sim Q \supset \sim P$
   $\sim Q$ $/ \therefore M$
   $\sim P$
   $R \cdot S$
   $(R \cdot S) \vee W$
   M

5. $\sim R \supset (A \cdot B)$
   $P \supset Q$
   $\sim Q \vee \sim S$
   $R \supset S$
   $\sim (A \cdot B)$ $/ \therefore \sim P$
   $(P \supset Q) \cdot (R \supset S)$
   $\sim P \vee \sim R$
   R
   $\sim P$

6. $\sim C \vee Q$
   $A \supset B$
   $Q \supset \sim S$
   S
   $B \supset C$ $/ \therefore \sim A$
   $\sim Q$
   $A \supset C$
   $\sim C$
   $\sim A$

7. $A \supset (P \supset Q)$
   $(P \supset R) \vee F$
   $A \cdot \sim F$
   $\sim Q \vee \sim R$ $/ \therefore \sim P$
   A
   $P \supset Q$
   $\sim F$
   $P \supset R$
   $(P \supset Q) \cdot (P \supset R)$
   $\sim P$

8. $A \supset B$
   $\sim A \supset (F \vee T)$
   $\sim F \cdot \sim D$
   $\sim B \vee C$
   $C \supset D$ $/ \therefore T$
   $\sim D$
   $\sim C$
   $\sim B$
   $\sim A$
   $F \vee T$
   $\sim F$
   T

9. $\sim B \vee \sim C$
   $\sim (A \vee Q) \supset B$
   $\sim P \supset C$
   $\sim P$ $/ \therefore (A \vee Q)$
   C
   $\sim B$
   $(A \vee Q)$

10. $\sim W$
    $\sim S \supset M$
    $S \supset P$
    $\sim M \vee W$ $/ \therefore P$
    $\sim M$
    S
    P

A LOOK AHEAD

The rules with which we have been working are somewhat limited. For example, consider the following argument:

$P \supset (R \vee S)$
$Q \supset P$
Q $/ \therefore S \vee R$
P *Modus Ponens*
$R \vee S$ *Modus Ponens*

The above argument is clearly valid, though our desired conclusion was $S \vee R$ and the actual conclusion was $R \vee S$. Strictly speaking, we did not justify this kind of move—our rules of inference did not provide for it. The move can be be justified, however, by invoking another general rule, according to which, *any expressions which are truth-functionally equivalent can be interchanged without change in truth value.* In order to justify the above conclusion, we would have to change $R \vee S$ into $S \vee R$. We can do this by invoking a truth-functional equivalence called *commutation.* This particular equivalence is of the general type

$p \vee q \equiv q \vee p$

Using this truth-functional equivalence, the correct representation of the above argument becomes:

$P \supset (R \vee S)$
$Q \supset P$
Q $/ \therefore S \vee R$
P *Modus Ponens*
$R \vee S$ *Modus Ponens*
$S \vee R$ *Commutation*

There are many truth-functional equivalences which can be of aid in justifying the steps of arguments. The following are among the most important:

Double Negation: $p \equiv \sim\sim p$
Tautology: $p \equiv (p \cdot p)$ and $p \equiv (p \vee p)$
Commutation: $(p \cdot q) \equiv (q \cdot p)$ and $(p \vee q) \equiv (q \vee p)$
Association: $[p \cdot (q \cdot r)] \equiv [(p \cdot q) \cdot r]$ and $[p \vee (q \vee r)] \equiv$
        $[(p \vee q) \vee r]$

Distribution: $p \cdot (q \vee r) \equiv (p \cdot q) \vee (p \cdot r)$ and $p \vee (q \cdot r) \equiv$
   $(p \vee q) \cdot (p \vee r)$
Transposition: $(p \supset q) \equiv (\sim q \supset \sim p)$
Implication: $(p \supset q) \equiv (\sim p \vee q) \equiv \sim (p \cdot \sim q)$
De Morgan's Theorems: $\sim (p \cdot q) \equiv (\sim p \vee \sim q)$ and $\sim (p \vee q) \equiv$
   $(\sim p \cdot \sim q)$
Exportation: $(p \cdot q) \supset r \equiv p \supset (q \supset r)$

EXERCISE 14.7

Show that the above are truth-functional equivalences by means of truth tables. If you need help, refer back to the section on disjunction.

Selected Readings

Ackermann, Robert, *Nondeductive Inference* (London, Routledge, 1966). This book offers a brief but good treatment of induction. A helpful bibliography appears at the end.

Barker, Stephen, *Elements of Logic* (New York, McGraw-Hill, 1966). Mr. Barker's treatment of quantification is one of the clearest introductions to the topic.

Beardsley, Monroe, *Thinking Straight* (Englewood Cliffs, New Jersey, Prentice-Hall, 1966). Some chapters offer a very good elucidation of the various uses and misuses of language.

Black, Max, *Critical Thinking* (Englewood Cliffs, New Jersey, Prentice-Hall, 1965). The third chapter clarifies some important points on the nature of validity. For some good tips on the different functions of language, the student should read all of the second part.

Carnap, Rudolf, *Logical Foundations of Probability* (Chicago, University of Chicago Press, 1962). Without a doubt one of the better treatments of the cluster of concepts which are relevant to an understanding of induction. The book is a must for all those who are interested in the meaning of "confirmation," "induction," and "probability."

Clark, Romane, and Paul Welsh, *Introduction to Logic* (Princeton, New Jersey, Van Nostrand, 1962). The last chapter is recommended as an interesting account of meaning and speech acts.

Copi, Irving, *Introduction to Logic* (New York, Macmillan, 1968). Mr. Copi has an excellent chapter on the various uses of language. His treatment of the connectives of symbolic logic is also laudable. But his presentation of quantification is not as good as Barker's, and his analysis of categorical propositions leaves much to be desired.

Copi, Irving, *Symbolic Logic* (New York, Macmillan, 1968). A clear and easily understood exposition of what is involved in a propositional calculus. The book has also an excellent section on the logic of relations. At its best it is a very useful introduction to some of the more advanced concepts of symbolic logic.

Dimnet, Ernest, *The Art of Thinking* (New York, Premier, 1964). A short and pleasurable book, which offers many practical hints on how to organize concepts in order to think effectively. Recommended for pleasure and profit.

Gianelli A. P., *Meaningful Logic* (Milwaukee, Bruce, 1962). The author clarifies many of the fundamental concepts of traditional logic. It is recommended for those who would like a clearer understanding of syllogistic reasoning.

Kneale, W., and M. Kneale, *The Development of Logic* (New York, Oxford University Press, 1964). This is one of the best histories of logic on the market. The student will find references to all the classics on logic.

Lemmon, E. J., *Beginning Logic* (London, Nelson & Sons, 1965). Very good as an introduction to symbolic logic. Especially valuable is Mr. Lemmon's clear analysis of identity. His exposition of quantification is also easily grasped.

Maritain, Jacques, *Formal Logic* (New York, Sheed & Ward, 1937). A very good presentation of some of the main concepts of traditional logic.

McGreal, Ian, *Analyzing Philosophical Arguments* (San Francisco, Chandler, 1967). Although not a logic text, the book is a good introduction to the analysis of philosophical problems. Valuable distinctions are made among different kinds of questions. As an unusual introduction to the criticism of philosophical argument, it is recommended to the student. The arguments analyzed are taken from such classics as Plato, Aristotle, Zeno, Berkeley, Descartes, and Mill.

Neidorf, Robert, *Deductive Forms* (New York, Harper & Row, 1967). The book has a clear presentation of the concept of validity. The chapter on quantification is rigorous and instructive.

Organ, T. W., *The Art of Critical Thinking* (Boston, Houghton Mifflin, 1965). One of the best texts on "practical" logic. The author's analysis of problem-solving techniques is very valuable. Mr. Organ gives some good hints on how to distinguish between recognizing a problem, what kind of problem we are dealing with, and stating problems clearly and usefully.

Quine, W. V. O., *Mathematical Logic* (New York, Harper & Row, 1962). This book, which is rather technical, is recommended mainly for those who are interested in the relationship between mathematics and logic. However, Chapters I and III offer very clear and readable expositions of what is involved in statements and terms. Professor Quine's section on the distinction between *use* and *mention* is valuable.

Quine, W. V. O., *Methods of Logic* (New York, Holt, Rinehart and Winston, Inc., 1966). Mr. Quine's book is the best introduction to the fundamental concepts of symbolic logic. His treatment of traditional logic is not as comprehensive as one would like, but this deficiency is more than compensated for by the originality and clarity with which most topics are presented. It is highly recommended for those who are interested in logic, mathematics, and ontology.

Robinson, Richard, *Definition* (Oxford, Clarendon, 1950). This is a small treasure of clarifications which are relevant to the concept of definition. The author's analysis of "real definition" is especially valuable.

Strawson, P. F., *Introduction to Logical Theory* (London, Methuen, 1950). An extremely lucid attempt to understand how the concepts of the logician function. The sixth chapter of the book illuminates a fundamental confusion which results from the failure to understand the nature of truth as manifested in categorical propositions. Mr. Strawson ably defends the traditional interpretation. The student should compare Strawson with Copi and Quine on the nature of truth. This book is highly recommended as "outside reading" for any introductory logic course.

Stebbing, L. S., *A Modern Introduction to Logic* (New York, Crowell, 1930). Although some of the terminology used in the book is obsolete, Miss Stebbing's historical sensitivity is responsible for some valuable distinctions which shed much light on the main differences (and similarities) between traditional and modern logic. Her explication of some modern ideas (especially her discussion of descriptions, which is fundamental to an understanding of the concept of truth as reformulated in *Principia Mathematica*) is unsurpassed in clarity.

Index